Beginner's Basque

with Online Audio

HIPPOCRENE BEGINNER'S SERIES

BEGINNER'S Basque

WITH ONLINE AUDIO

Wim Jansen

HIPPOCRENE BOOKS, INC.
NEW YORK

Acknowledgments

I am greatly indebted to Dr. Rudolf De Rijk and Dr. Yves D'Hulst (both of Leyden University, The Netherlands) for their scrupulous review of parts of the manuscript of this book and for their many valuable suggestions. I also wish to thank Aitor Arana from Azpeitia (Basque Country) for his meticulous review of all draft material and for the support he has given me as a native speaker of the language.

Audio files available at www.hippocrenebooks.com

Online audio edition, 2018
1st paperback-with-audio edition 2007

ISBN 978-0-7818-1378-5
Previous edition ISBN: 978-0-7818-1227-6

For information, address:
Hippocrene Books, Inc.
171 Madison Avenue
New York, NY 10016

www.hippocrenebooks.com

Printed in the United States of America.

CONTENTS

Audio files available for download at:
http://www.hippocrenebooks.com/beginners-online-audio.html

INTRODUCTION

Despite the fact that the Basque language or *euskara* has been in use for more than 2000 years in the area where it is still spoken today, politically speaking it is a language without a home. What we call the Basque Country (*País Vasco* in Spanish, *Pays Basque* in French, *Euskal Herria* in Basque) is a traditional geographical concept and not a political definition.[1] It comprises three regions in France and four in Spain, all clustered around the lower corner of the Bay of Biscay and divided in the middle by the French-Spanish national border. The area where Basque is spoken today lies well within these seven regions. It extends for about 160 kilometers (100 miles) from west to east, from the city of Bilbao to the mountain peak of the Pic d'Anie in the Pyrenees, and for about 50 kilometers (30 miles) from north to south, from the city of Bayonne to just north of the city of Pamplona. In the absence of any public protection, Basque never reached the status of official language in its entire history. Basque slowly developed into a literary language, later than other languages around it. The first printed book in Basque was not published until 1545.

Latin and its Romance descendant languages in and around the Basque Country were the natural sources from which priests, lawyers, and merchants retrieved the names for the new concepts and products that were gradually introduced into the traditional rural society. Indeed, borrowing terms from neighboring languages goes back to the days of classical Latin, as we can still hear in such words as *bake* for 'peace' and *lege* for 'law', in which the original velar sounds of *pacem* and *legem* from classical Latin persist. In the wake of Latin, French and Spanish became the most important suppliers not only of new words, but also of non-Basque sentence constructions, accents, and intonations. Even modern terms in the field of computer technology often enter Basque through a French or Spanish filter.

The lack of a politically unified nation and of a cultural center

[1] For easy recognition Basque geographical entities are quoted in French or Spanish depending on where they are located, with the proper Basque designation added in brackets. English names are used when available, e.g. Labourd (Lapurdi), Vizcaya (Bizkaia), Navarre (Nafarroa).

like Paris or Florence has contributed to the persistence of different regional varieties which, divided and unsheltered as they were, have been exposed to heavy pressures from the state-supported French and Spanish throughout Basque history. According to classifications made in the 19th and early 20th centuries, the Basque-speaking area was divided into six to nine major dialects among which we quote Bizkaian, Guipuzkoan, High Navarrese (all three spoken in Spain) and Lapurdian, Low Navarrese, and Zuberoan (spoken in France), with more subdivisions possible.[2] The Roncalese dialect, still present in the 19th century descriptions, is now extinct. The most recent investigations (1997) show that over the last fifty years the different dialects have been growing closer to each other and that no more than five distinct regional versions of Basque can be identified. This is not only the result of the increased mobility of the population and of the improved means of communication. In the past, regional dialects and local varieties with a host of competing forms of meaning and spelling co-existed and proliferated without much control. Today, there is a strong unifying force exerted on the language by the Basque Academy, the mass media, and the public education system in the Spanish part of the Basque Country. Much of this is to the credit of the government of the Basque Autonomous Community. The recent creation of *euskara batua*, the unified literary language for all Basque-speaking people, makes it easier to stand up against pressures from outside. Under the umbrella of the decreed *euskara batua* the individual regional varieties of Basque can blossom as the vehicles of regional and local cultural expressions, in literature, theater, and music. The defense of Basque as a minority language has thus been taken over by *euskara batua*.

The Basque language shows a large number of characteristics that are totally alien to its Indo-European environment. This marks it without any shade of doubt as a language of different origin. It remains a mystery, however, where or when the language originated, which prehistorical migrations it took part in, and where any possible relatives might be found. Many attempts have

[2] Basque dialect designations are given as anglicized versions of the original Basque names, except where proper English names are readily available, e.g. Bizkaian (from Bizkaiera), but Roncalese and Navarrese.

been made to relate Basque to Celtic languages, to Finnish and its Asian relatives, to languages from northern Africa and from the Caucasian area and even to certain Indian languages of the American continent. Probably no single feature of Basque is so unique that it cannot be found somewhere else among the thousands of languages that populate the world, but no consistent pattern of coincidences has been discovered yet. Even if such a pattern would be traced, it would require supporting non-linguistic evidence in the form of archaeological or anthropological data to establish a truly genealogical relationship rather than a typological similarity. And since no breakthrough in this field is expected soon, the mystery of Basque is bound to stay unrevealed.

History of the Basque People and Their Language

Basque predates Indo-European languages: Prehistory to the First Invasions

The Basque Country has been inhabited since the Paleolithic period, as is demonstrated by the mural paintings preserved in numerous limestone caves in the area.

According to most scholars some form of Basque was spoken as early as the second millennium B.C., in an area much vaster than what is nowadays referred to as the Basque Country. The triangle enclosed by the Bay of Biscay, the river Garonne, and the mountain chain of the Pyrenees is defined as the historical northern territory of Basque, known as Aquitaine. The land that stretches across and to the south of the mountains until the river Ebro and to the west until the Cantabrian mountains is its historical southern territory. This statement is supported by the distribution of Basque-sounding geographical names, the location of tombstones with inscriptions reminiscent of Basque names, and by extra-linguistic information such as the distribution of blood groups among the population in and around these historical Basque-speaking territories.

The Basque language is the last living language in western Europe that dates back to the days before the Indo-European immigration: it has survived all subsequent invasions of the Indo-European languages like Latin and its modern successors French and Spanish.

In the first millennium before our era Celtic tribes settled in the southern part of the area. They were the first Indo-Europeans to move into the Basque Country. The Basque language as we know it today bears only minimal marks of any Celtic influence that may have been the result of this contact.

Latin influence on Basque begins: Roman Times until Middle Ages

In the second century B.C. the first Roman settlers arrived in the south of the Basque Country. This was the beginning of a long period of Latin influence on Basque. The northern territory of Aquitaine was conquered by Caesar during his Gallic war (56 B.C.). During the Roman occupation Latin was widely used in the area. After the fall of the empire the local forms of Latin gradually broke up and developed into the Romance languages, which are still prevalent in and around the Basque Country: Gascon, the Langue d'oc, and the Langue d'oïl (French) in France, and Castilian (Spanish) in Spain.

In the 5th century Visigoths wandered through the area, but they were later pushed back by the Franks to the Mediterranean coast and into the Iberian peninsula. By the 6th century the duchy of Gascony was formed under Frankish control. Until the 8th century local Basque leaders defied the Frankish and later more specifically Carolingian authorities, which resulted in frequent conflicts and wars between the competing powers. The famous battle of Roncevaux or Roncesvalles (in Basque: Orreaga) in the year 778, during which Charlemagne's rearguard under Roland was annihilated by the Basques, reminds us of those turbulent times.

In 796 the Basques north of the Pyrenees were subdued by Charlemagne and the dukes of Gascony remained under Carolingian control. From the beginning of the 9th century and in a move to loosen its links with the Carolingian rulers, the north reoriented its sphere of interest towards the Basque kingdom of Pamplona (later: Navarre), just to its south. However, in the beginning of the 11th century the coastal region of Labourd and the more inland Soule were detached from Navarre and later fell back into the hands of the duke of Aquitaine. From then on until the 15th century the fate of the northern territory was closely linked to the developments in France and Navarre. For some time, following Eleanor of Aquitaine's marriage to the duke of Normandy in 1152, parts of the territory (roughly: Labourd and Soule) came under the domination of the crown of England.

Basque under French and Spanish rule: The Middle Ages until the Mid-Nineteenth Century

At the end of the Hundred Years' War (1453) Labourd and Soule became parts of France. The central area of Basse-Navarre continued to be part of the kingdom of Navarre until it became French in the 16th century. From this date onwards the northern territory belonged to France and its further development was to be determined by the court and administration in Paris.

After the 9th century the peninsular Basques to the west of the kingdom of Navarra began to develop states of their own, forming the territories of Álava, Vizcaya, and Guipúzcoa. Between the late 11th and the 14th centuries these territories were gradually incorporated into the kingdom of Castile, though in practice they retained a fair amount of autonomy through the *fueros* or 'charters' that were granted to them by the Crown. Castilian was the official language, and Basque maintained a status of regional language. In 1515 the kingdom of Navarre underwent the same fate as the other Basque territories in the south and was absorbed by Castile.

Under King Francis I in 1539 French became the one and only official language in the northern territories of the Basque Country, to the detriment of Basque. After the French Revolution all privileges enjoyed by the local Basque communities were abolished. The same thing happened in Spain during the course of the 19th century when the Basques were defeated twice by the central government forces in the so-called Carlist Wars (1833–1839 and 1873–1876).

The beginning of Basque nationalism: The Late Nineteenth Century

During the awakening of modern nationalism in Europe, the struggle for the preservation of Basque became part of the social and political opposition to the centralist governments that ruled from Paris and Madrid (1876–1936). Sabino Arana (1865–1903) is often called the father of Basque nationalism. As a journalist and politician he devoted much of his life to writing and lecturing about the need for a reasserted Basque identity. In 1886 he wrote: "The Basque language is the essential element of the Basque nation and without it our national institutions are inconceivable." Arana designed the flag that became the national flag of all Basques: a double green and white cross on a red background, known as the *ikurriña*. Already in 1853 the wandering bard José

María Iparraguirre had composed the hymn *Gernikako Arbola* (The tree of Guernica), which became the Basque national anthem.

Numerous historical documents from this period show that the very survival of the Basque language was at stake, as is eloquently illustrated by a statement issued by the prefect of the department of Basses-Pyrénées in 1846: "It is a special task of our schools in the Basque Country to replace the Basque language with French." The statement was typical of the official attitude towards the Basque language on both sides of the national border, calling for the elimination of any form of teaching of Basque and the suppression of all cultural expressions.

Although the Basque resistance movement against the overt oppression had been politically organized since 1895, a demand for Basque autonomy was not formulated until the early 1930s, i.e. during the Second Spanish Republic.

The Basque language and the Spanish Civil War: The Early to Mid-Twentieth Century

In 1919 the Basque language academy was founded under the name of *Euskaltzaindia*, which literally means 'The society of guardians of Basque'. From then on the fight for recognition became more serious and at the same time more prestigious. Unfortunately, the initial activities of the academy were brutally interrupted by the outbreak of the Spanish civil war (1936–1939). The end of the war, during which the majority of Basques fought on the losing side, marked the beginning of a period during which the Basque movement was basically paralyzed. It was not until 1956 that the first public meeting of the academy was held. Since 1968 the academy has been instrumental in creating and promoting the unified Basque language or *euskara batua*.

During the entire Franco period in Spain the use of the Basque language and any expression of Basque culture were obstructed—if not forbidden—and it was only after Franco's death and the establishment of a modern democracy in Spain that Basque was rehabilitated. It is, therefore, not surprising that in 1953 a group of students from Bilbao set up a pro-Basque discussion forum which they called *Ekin* (meaning something like 'get on with it' or 'get down to it'). This rapidly expanding group of youngsters grew more and more restless and militant over the years, until it reorganized itself in 1959 and gave itself the new and self-explanatory name of *Euskadi Ta Askatasuna* ('Basque Country and Freedom'), abbreviated ETA. Euskadi, another expression for Basque Country, originated as an erroneously created neologism of the 19th century and is a term laden with political connotations.

In the 1960s the Basque language and culture re-emerged as the pressure from the fascist authorities in Spain began to diminish. *Ikastolak* (schools with Basque as the primary language) sprang up everywhere and movements to promote adult literacy in Basque were created. The definitive rehabilitation of Basque came with the institution in Spain of a modern constitutional monarchy in the mid-1970s. In 1976 the Basque academy was bequeathed the epithet 'royal,' so that nowadays, at least in Spanish, it is referred to as the *Real Academia de la Lengua Vasca* ('Royal Academy of the Basque Language'). The academy has ordinary members, corresponding members, and honorary members, and it regularly publishes its proceedings in Basque with contributions in Spanish and French.

The creation of the Basque Autonomous Community: The 1970s and 1980s

Article 3 of the Spanish constitution of 1978 opened the door to the official recognition of Basque in the newly created Basque Autonomous Community (Álava, Vizcaya, and Guipúzcoa), in accordance with the statute of autonomy that was to be passed to this region in 1979. The statute defines Basque as an official language in the Basque Autonomous Community (*Euskal Herriko Autonomia Erkidegoa*), together with Spanish. It stipulates that all inhabitants of the region have the right to know and use both languages and it guarantees the use of both languages by the public institutions. It also prohibits discrimination on the grounds of language.

In 1982 Basque was given the status of official language in the Basque-speaking areas of the autonomous province of Navarre (which is not part of the Basque Autonomous Community). In 1986 the Navarrese parliament divided the territory into three different areas: Basque-speaking, non-Basque-speaking, and mixed, with different degrees of recognition for Basque in each.

Both in the Basque Autonomous Community and in the Basque-speaking areas of Navarre, pre-university teaching is an option in either Basque or Spanish, with the other language taught as a separate subject. Mixed teaching is the third option. The University of the Basque Country has Basque and Spanish as its official languages.

In 1982 a public body was set up in the Basque Autonomous Community that became responsible for two television channels, one of them broadcasting entirely in Basque, and a number of radio stations, among which two are in Basque. The amount of Basque used by local stations reflects the percentage of Basque speakers in their municipalities.

A modern survey of Basque: The 1990s

In 2001, the Third Sociolinguistic Survey of the Basque Country was carried out, following earlier surveys done in 1991 and 1996. As with the earlier surveys, the 2001 survey was aimed at an in-depth study of the sociolinguistic situation in the Basque Country, the natural transmission of the language through the family, the incorporation into the society of new speakers of Basque who had acquired Basque as a second language, and the attitude of the population towards measures to promote the use of Basque. According to the data collected in this survey, 24.7% of the population in the French Basque Country was bilingual, 29.4% in the Basque Autonomous Community in Spain, and only 10.3% in the province of Navarre. In other words, about one-quarter of the population in the north and almost one-third in the Autonomous Community speak Basque. This number is about one out of ten in the province of Navarre.

The all-time low of the number of speakers of Basque was reached in 1981. Since then the numbers are rising again in the Autonomous Community and remain unchanged in Navarre. However, in the north the decline continues. For the whole of the

Basque Country, the 2001 survey established approximately 634,000 people of the age of sixteen and above who were conversant in Basque. Bilingual speakers use more Basque than French or Spanish in the family circle, in their local environment (among friends and colleagues, in the stores and at the market, in the church) and in certain formal environments like the town hall and the local bank office.

In France the language continues to survive under difficult circumstances as a regional language with little or no recognition. No institutional support is available, and French remains the only officially recognized language. Some optional teaching of Basque at pre-university levels is possible, but French is the single official language in education, used in exams, for theses, and in reports issued by private and public educational establishments.

In a way, the linguistic and cultural renaissance that has taken place in the Spanish part of the Basque Country during the last quarter of the 20th century has given the Basque language a position and prestige it probably never held in history. Nevertheless, continued political tension and the waves of violence that harass the area cast a shadow on this process and pose a threat to its undisturbed further development.

The Basque Country Today

Geography

The Basque Country is situated in the southwest of Europe along the Spanish-French border near the Bay of Biscay. Along its northern borders in France are the Landes and Béarn regions and to its south in Spain is the province of Rioja. To the west of the Basque Country in Spain are the provinces of Castile and Cantabria, to the east and southeast Aragón. The Basque Country covers a surface area of about 20,864 square kilometers (8050 square miles, about the size of the state of Massachusetts) and numbers a population of almost 2.9 million people (reference data 1995). The country lies in the Central European time zone (Greenwich Mean Time + 1 hour) and switches to and from daylight saving time together with the other European countries.

The Basque Country is composed of seven different historical regions, three of them situated in France and four in Spain. Going from the coast inland and following the national border in an easterly direction, we cross the French regions of Labourd (*Lapurdi*), Basse-Navarre (*Nafarroa Beherea*), and Soule (*Zuberoa*), with a total of 249,000 inhabitants (1990 census). These three regions represent historical units only. From an administrative point of view they are currently part of the department of the Pyrénées Atlantiques, with its capital city Pau located outside the historical Basque land.

The four Basque regions in Spain are Vizcaya (*Bizkaia*), Álava (*Araba*), Guipúzcoa (*Gipuzkoa*), and Navarra (*Nafarroa*), the latter one known in English as Navarre. The former three are administrative units called provinces and form together the Basque Autonomous Community (*Euskal Herriko Autonomia Erkidegoa*) with 2.1 million inhabitants (1991 census). The province of Navarre has a special, separate status and counted just over 523,000 inhabitants in the 1991 census.

The seven regions together make up the Basque Country or *Euskal Herria* in Basque, i.e. the land where the Basque language is spoken, and not a sovereign state in the modern legal sense of the word. Their cultural unity is symbolized by the device in their common coat of arms: *Zazpiak Bat* 'Seven in One'.

The main cities in the Basque Country are the historical capitals of Bayonne (*Baiona*), Saint Jean-Pied-de-Port (*Donibane Garazi*), and Mauléon-Lixarre (*Maule-Lextarre*) in the north and the provincial capitals of Bilbao (*Bilbo*), San Sebastián (*Donostia*), Vitoria (*Gasteiz*), and Pamplona (*Iruñea*) in the south. Vitoria is the capital of the Basque Autonomous Community, whereas Pamplona may be called the historical capital of the Basque Country as a whole. Founded by the Romans, it was the capital of the kingdom of Navarre during the Middle Ages and as such became the center of maximum Basque expansion during the 11th century. Biarritz (*Miarritze*) in Labourd is a mundane seaside resort and Guernica (*Gernika*) in Vizcaya is known not only for its ancient Vizcayan parliament building, but more recently for its destruction by Nazi bombers during the Spanish Civil War, the event behind Picasso's *Guernica*.

Nature and climate

Wide sandy beaches stretch along the northern French coastline of the country, becoming a ragged rocky coast with high and steep cliffs near the chain of the Pyrenees. The mountains that run from west to east reach heights from about 900 meters (2950 feet) near the coast in Labourd (La Rhune) to more than 2500 meters (8200 feet) in Soule (Pic d'Anie). To the north of the mountains gentle green hills stretch out until the flat land near and beyond the river Adour. Much of the Basque Country is covered with forests, with pine and eucalyptus woods dominating in Vizcaya and Guipúzcoa. Navarre and the mountainous regions on the French side of the national border are famous for their dense oak woods. Because of the rich vegetation, green remains the dominant color to the south of the mountains also, i.e. in the provinces of Vizcaya, Guipúzcoa, and the upper part of Navarre. However, as we move south and away from the ocean, the scenery changes. Much of the area is a high plateau with yellow and brown as the dominant colors until the narrow green valley of the river Ebro.

The mountainous parts of the Basque Country have numerous caves, many of which are archaeological sites that preserve traces of human presence, like mural paintings, from thousands of years ago. The best known caves are those of Isturitz, Oxocelhaya, and Sare on the French side, and Santimamiñe, Ekain, and Solacueva on the Spanish side. Other traces of human occupation that have become part of the natural scenery are the dolmens or megalithic burial mounds to be found particularly in the mountainous areas of Álava and Navarre.

In the French part of the Basque Country, the summers are less hot than along the other coast of southern France, the Mediterranean, but the winters are mild compared to other parts of France. There is considerable rainfall in the area, especially in some of the mountainous regions and in the hinterland just behind the coast. Relatively warm winds blowing down from the mountains may cause mild temperatures at times when other parts of the continent are cooler. The Spanish part of the Basque Country close to the ocean has a climate that is very similar to the climate in the French part. The southernmost areas of Álava and Navarre, however, feature a continental climate with hot summers and cold winters.

Economy

The northern regions of Labourd, Basse-Navarre, and Soule are far away from any main industrial center in France and their economies continue to be built on agriculture, fishing and associated activities. Tourism has also become an important factor, particularly by wealthy people from places up to hundreds of miles away who built their second homes in the Basque countryside. The agricultural sector and its associated processing industries produce vegetables, corn, wheat, potatoes, honey, dairy products, wine, and a number of excellent cow and sheep cheeses. In the Southern Basque Country corn and wheat are grown. Here too, local processing yields some excellent sheep cheeses and wine grapes are important in the southernmost parts of Navarre and Álava. Along the coast of the Southern Basque Country fishing is as important as it is in the north.

The provinces of Vizcaya and Guipúzcoa are heavily industrialized. The metallurgical industry has an old tradition in the area, with steel plants, shipyards, and production facilities for machinery and tools. Other examples of industrial activity are the paper factories along the many rivers that cross the country from the south to the north, the manufacturing of electric appliances, and the processing of canned food. Tourism is important here as well, especially in the coastal areas (fishing and swimming) and in the mountains (trekking, rafting, and mountaineering).

The Basque Country has a well-developed internal network of roads and highways and is linked by high-capacity tollways to the big cities of Bordeaux, Toulouse, Burgos, Zaragoza, and Madrid. There are high-speed train links with Paris (TGV) and Madrid and each of the major Basque cities has an airport with many domestic and international connections.

Until 2002 the legal currencies in the Basque Country were the French franc in the north and the Spanish peseta in the south. Starting from January 1, 2002, the euro is the single currency in both parts of the country.

Politics

The *legebiltzarra* or parliament of the Basque Autonomous Community exercises the legislative power in the Community, monitors the actions of the Basque government, and approves its budgets. The parliament is elected by the Basque people in a direct ballot every four years. It has seventy-five members equally divided among the historical territories of Álava, Vizcaya, and Guipúzcoa. Parliamentary elections take place in each of these areas according to the principle of proportional representation. During the legislation that started with the 1998 elections, the administration was ultimately led by a minority coalition between two moderate nationalist groups, the Basque Nationalist Party (PNV) and the Basque Union (EA), holding only twenty-seven of the seventy-five seats. The remaining seats were divided among four more parties including the militant Basque Nationalists or Euskal Herritarrok (EH), holding fourteen seats. The EH (later to be known as the Batasuna Party) was the political arm of the ETA, a paramilitary political group demanding Basque independence that has committed violent acts to achieve its ends. In 2002, Spain passed a law banning political parties that support violence—including the ETA and, in 2003, the Batasuna. The elections of May 2001, which were necessary because of the lack of governing power of the leading coalition, resulted in a crushing victory of the moderate nationalists (PNV–EA) against the radicals who lost half their seats in parliament. However, the elections of 2005 saw something of a resurgence of radical nationalism: the moderate PNV-EA alliance won again, but only by a small margin, while the Communist party of the Basque Land (PCTV), a political party with no former representation in the Autonomous Basque Parliament, gained nine seats (12.44% of the votes). The PCTV had opened its party lists to accommodate voters of the Batasuna Party, when Batasuna was outlawed in 2003 for its ties to the violent ETA.

The *jaurlaritza* or government consists of the president, vice-president, and ten councillors. The president or *lehendakaria* is elected by the parliament. The 1998–2001 government was headed by Mr. Juan José Ibarretxe Markuartu of the PNV, who returned after the May 2001 elections with more solid support than before. Ibarretxe was again elected president by the parliament after the May 2005 elections, though the PNV-EA coalition backing him won fewer seats than in the previous election. The seat of the government and the parliament is in Vitoria (*Gasteiz*). Respecting a tradition of centuries, the *lehendakaria* is sworn into office under the oak in front of the Vizcayan parliament building in Guernica (*Gernika*).

The Basque Autonomous Community is represented in the parliament of Spain in Madrid. Among the 350 members of the House of Representatives nineteen are from the Community in accordance with the following key: four from Álava, nine from Vizcaya, and six from Guipúzcoa. Of the 207 members of the Spanish Senate, twelve represent the Basque Autonomous Community.

Some Aspects of the Basque Culture

Literature

Compared with other languages in Europe, written literature in Basque appeared only recently. It is interesting to note that the first printed book in Basque was published outside the Basque Country (in Bordeaux) and under a Latin title: *Linguae Vasconum Primitiae* (1545). It contained poetry written by Bernard Etxepare in the Low-Navarrese dialect. The first translation of the New Testament was prepared by the Calvinist Leizarraga and appeared in 1571 in a mix of northern dialects. The first grammar (of the Guipuzcoan dialect) was written by Larramendi; its title in Spanish, *El Imposible Vencido* (The impossible overcome), reveals how difficult it must have been to make the first comprehensive description of the complex Basque language. Nowadays good textbooks and dictionaries exist, most of them in Basque, Spanish, or French, with some material that has recently become available in other languages like Dutch, English, Hungarian, and Russian.

After centuries of poverty, in terms of scope and numbers, it was only in the 1950s that a true literary production in Basque made a cautious start under the slowly fading pressure that was exerted by the Franco regime. Reprints of the few classical works of real importance became available, such as *Gero* (by Axular) and *Peru Abarka* (by Moguel). During the second half of the century fiction writing in Basque, both in prose and poetry, developed along the lines of national reassertion and social commitment towards a form of artistic expression in its own right. At the beginning of the 21st century Basque literature shows itself as fully developed and diversified in its thematic coverage. Basque writers, however, are not yet well known beyond the borders of their small country, with the exception of Bernardo Atxaga, whose *Obabakoak* (Stories from Obaba) has been translated into many languages. The popular Book Fair of Durango (in the province of Vizcaya) was inaugurated in 1965 and brings together scores of publishers for many thousands of visitors each year. Book production in the Basque Country increased fifty times between 1950 and 1990.

Music and dance

A flute cut from the bone of a bird and found in the cave of Isturitz dates back to prehistorical times and proves the antiquity of this particular instrument in the musical history of the Basque country. The popular three-hole flute called *txistua* is indeed one of the classical musical instruments of the Basques, together with the small drum or *danbolina*. The mixture of their sounds accompanies the *mascarades*, open-air theater plays and dance performances in the country.

Singing is a very popular and well-developed art and pastime among the Basques and sung epical poetry belongs to the oldest known melodies of the country. Choral music is widespread and there are at least fifty choirs in the north alone. The first modern singer in Basque is Michel Labèguérie (1921–1980), whose expression of pro-Basque sentiments was clearly influenced by the nationalist movement in nearby Catalonia. From the mid-1960s popular folk singers and groups made their appearance and they influenced the development and spread of literary Basque, be it through new compositions or through the revival of ancient poetry in a new musical setting. Names worth mentioning are: Mikel Laboa, Benito Lertxundi, Txomin Artola, Olatz Zugasti, and the famous band Oskorri (Red dawn).

Poets or bards called *bertsolariak* (verse makers) are famous for their instant poetry. Challenged on the spot to respond to a given theme, their improvizations have to be in strict compliance with a prescribed metric. Market place rallies and nationwide championships attract thousands of fans and admirers and the most capable *bertsolariak* rank among the best known national figures.

There is hardly any place in the Basque country that does not have its own type of dance, performed by semi-professional or amateur groups whenever there is a local or regional festival, procession, or fair. Most of them are sparkling shows of music, motion, colors, and costumes. Some dances, performed at high speed and involving different kinds of hand-held objects or obstacles on the floor, require a fair amount of physical strength and acrobatic talent from the performers. Perhaps the best known dances are the *aurreskua* (performed by male dancers and accompanied by flutes and drums), the *godalet dantza* (a dance around a drinking glass without toppling it), the *ezpata dantza* or sword dance, the *bordon dantza* where the dancers perform swinging maneuvers with long wooden sticks, and many more…

Sports

Apart from the sports found all over the world like soccer and tennis, there are typical Basque sports that enjoy great popularity. Most of these sports have their origin in the hard physical work of the farmers, shepherds, foresters, and fishermen of the ancient Basque society and combine a display of sheer physical strength with elements of astuteness and competition. *Aizkolariak* or 'woodcutters' are the sportive descendants of the foresters, whose job it is to cut through a log of wood as fast as they can. The *harrijasotzaileak* or 'stone lifters' are the Basque version of our Olympic weightlifters and remind us of the workers in the quarries. Dragging a heavy stone across the field faster than your competitor is what is done during the so-called *gizon proba* or 'men's test'. In some sports domestic or farm animals are employed, e.g. in the *idi proba* or 'test of the oxen', where huge stones are dragged by the owner's ox rather than by the farmer himself. The *soka tira* or 'tug of war' and rowboat races or regattas remind us of the long naval history of the Basques when explorers, whalers, merchants, and fishermen sailed on all oceans.

The best known Basque sport, however, is the *pilota* or *pelota*, known in the United States in the version called *jai alai* or 'joyful game'. *Pilota* has its roots in medieval ball games whereby the players used the naked hand to hit the ball. Through the centuries, the Basques have transformed this old game into a modern and thrilling sport. It is played by teams on fields and in indoor courts, but requires in any case one vertical wall (*frontoia*) against which the ball (*pilota*) must be hit before it bounces back on the ground, to be hit back against the wall by the adversary team. The ball is either smashed by the naked hand, which is the original way the game was played, or by some device to protect the hand and to increase the power that is given to the ball. Leather gloves can be used, but also the impressive, oblong reed launching baskets (*txis-*

tera), wooden bats or even rackets with soft or stretched cords. *Pilota* is the national sport of the Basques and a *frontoia* can be found even in the tiniest and remotest corner of the country.

Gastronomy

The Basque Country is renowned for its excellent cuisine, particularly its seafood, fresh fish, and crustaceans of the best imaginable quality and cooked in a variety of manners. Beef, lamb, and other meat are highly appreciated alternatives to the seafood. Especially in the southern part of the country, cold and hot appetizers are often meals in their own right and served in overcrowded bars between noontime and 2 p.m.

The country offers a wide choice of top quality natural foods like vegetables and dairy products. Noteworthy among the cheeses is the characteristic round and deep yellow *Idiazabal*, a tasty sheep cheese from Guipúzcoa. Genuine Basque wines are the red and rosé Irouléguy (*Irulegi*) from Basse-Navarre and the white Chacolí (*Txakolina*) from the Guipúzcoan and Vizcayan coastal areas. As a sweet finishing touch the Gâteau Basque (cake with cream or cherry filling) should not be missed.

Abbreviations and Symbols

The following abbreviations and symbols are used in this book.

lit.	literally
>	gives, produces
<	derives from
/.../	key to the pronunciation

ALPHABET AND PRONUNCIATION

The Basque alphabet consists of the same letters as the English alphabet plus the letter *ñ* which follows the letter *n* and precedes the *o*. The letters *c*, *q*, *v*, *w*, and *y* are only used in loan words that retain their foreign spelling. These letters do not occur in words of genuine Basque origin. There can be big differences in pronunciation between one dialect and the other. The following global guidelines apply to the *euskara batua* or 'Unified Basque', the standard language used in most of the newly published literature, in the mass media, and at school.

Vowels

Basque has a simple system of five vowels written as *a*, *e*, *i*, *o*, and *u*. Their pronunciation is relatively short and clear, without the glide into a diphthong that is so characteristic of many English vowels. Basically, the properties of a vowel do not vary with its place of occurrence in a word. Therefore, vowel reduction or loss of its characteristic sound in unstressed positions does not exist in Basque. Each vowel, and therefore each syllable, is pronounced clearly and distinctly.

Vowel	Approximate Pronunciation	Transcription	Example
a	*ah as in* ***fa****ther*	/a/	alaba /alaba/ *daughter*
e	*eh as in* ***e****gg*	/e/	eme /eme/ *female*
i	*ee as in d****ee****p*	/i/	niri /niri/ *to me*
o	*oh as in n****o****t*	/o/	oro /oro/ *all*
u	*oo as in b****oo****k*	/u/	buru /buru/ *head*

Diphthongs

A diphthong is a fixed sequence of a vowel preceded or followed by another short vowel with which it forms a single pronunciation unit. The six diphthongs in Basque are:

Diphthong	Approximate pronunciation	Transcription	Example
au	*ow as in* ***cow***	/aw/	gau /gaw/ *night*
eu	*eh-oo pronounced quickly*	/ew/	zeu /sew/ *yourself*
ai	*y as in m**y***	/ay/	bai /bay/ *yes*
ei	*eh-ee pronounced quickly*	/ey/	dei /dey/ *call*
oi	*oy as in b**oy***	/oy/	oin /oyn/ *foot*
ui	*oo-ee pronounced quickly*	/uy/	muin /muyn/ *marrow*

The letters *w* and *y* are used in this transcription to represent the semi-vowels with which these diphthongs end.

Consonants

The consonants written as *b*, *d*, *f*, *k*, *l*, *m*, *n*, *p*, and *t* are pronounced as in English. It should be noted, however, that a strong stop consonant like *p*, *t*, or *k* before a vowel is never aspirated. The Basque word for 'tea', *te*, is pronounced /te/ and not /tʰe/, where the ʰ stands for the characteristic short puff that can be heard in the English 'tea' /tʰi/. The remaining consonants display characteristics that are illustrated in the following table. As will be seen in this table, the pronunciation of the written *j* is sometimes that of a consonant and sometimes that of a semi-vowel, depending on the dialect. For reasons of simplicity the *j* is classified under the consonants below.

Consonant	Pronunciation	Transcription	Example
g	*always like the English g in **go***	/g/	gu /gu/ *we*
h	*aspirated in the northern Basque Country, else-where mute*	/h/	hura /(h)ura/ *that*
j	*like y in **y**es, but with local variants like the Spanish jota in Juan (John) or the French j in journal (newspaper)*	/j/	jan /jan/ *to eat*
ñ	*identical to the Spanish ñ in ma**ñ**ana (tomorrow) or the English ny in ca**ny**on*	/ny/	andereño /anderenyo/ *young lady*
r	*represents a light flap just like the Spanish single r in pe**r**o (but)*	/r/	gure /gure/ *our*
rr	*has the prolonged trill like the Spanish double rr in pe**rr**o (dog)*	/rr/	berri /berri/ *new*
s	*a voiceless palatal s, that most closely resem-bles the English sh, with the tongue-tip touching the forward hard palate or alveolar ridge*	/s'/	su /s'u/ *fire*
x	*like the English sh in **sh**ip but with unrounded lips*	/sh/	xagu /shagu/ *little mouse*
z	*like the voiceless English s but with the tongue-tip bent downwards*	/s/	zuri /suri/ *white*

The last three friction sounds form so-called affricates when preceded by the voiceless stop *t*. They are written *ts*, *tx*, and *tz* and are all voiceless. The point of articulation of the frictional part (*s*, *x*, or *z*) is not affected by the *t*.

Consonant cluster	***Pronunciation***	***Transcription***	***Example***
ts	*t followed by palatal s tending towards the English ch in* ***ch****ip*	/ts'/	hots /(h)ots'/ *noise*
tx	*like the English ch in* ***ch****ip*	/tsh/	etxe /etshe/ *house*
tz	*like the English ts in bi****ts***	/ts/	hitz /(h)its/ *word*

Further notes on consonants

Between vowels, the voiced stops *b*, *d*, and *g* develop into their frictional counterparts with *b* tending towards the English 'w' without rounding the lips, *d* towards the English voiced 'th' in '**th**at', and *g* towards a voiced variant of the Scottish 'ch' in 'lo**ch**'. These shifts are not represented in our transcription.

The *n*-sound in the middle of words assimilates to a following stop and becomes *m* before *b* and *ng* before *k*:

> *zenbat* (how much) is pronounced /sembat/ due to *nb* > /mb/
> *hanka* (leg) is pronounced /(h)angka/ due to *nk* > /ngk/

The *r*-sound cannot occur at the beginning of a word. Loan words that would have an initial *r* insert a vowel in front of them: the Latin or Italian *Roma* becomes *Erroma* in Basque, Latin *rosa* (rose) becomes *arrosa* in Basque, with a consistent reduplication in the spelling (trilled *r*).

The *l* and *n* sounds when preceded by the vowel *i* and followed by a vowel are palatalized (softened), i.e. pronounced like the 'lli' in 'mi**lli**on' or the 'ny' in 'ca**ny**on'. In our transcription we use the letter *y* to indicate the palatalization of a consonant (see above for the pronunciation of the Basque letter *ñ*).

mila (a thousand) is pronounced /milya/ because of the *l* between *i* and *a*.
ilun (dark) is pronounced /ilyun/ because of the *l* between *i* and *u*.

This effect also occurs when the preceding *i* is the semi-vowel of a diphthong:

maila (step or level) sounds like /malya/, and
soinu (music) sounds like /s'onyu/,

i.e. the consonant is palatalized and the preceding diphthong turns into a vowel.

Where an intervocalic *h* is dropped in the pronunciation, particularly in the southern part of the Basque Country, the resultant combination of two vowels tends to become a diphthong: *behia* (the cow) will then sound like /beya/, and *ohitura* (the habit) like /oytura/.

Word accent (stress) and intonation

There are many regional and local variations, but in general, accentuation in Basque is weak. Place the stress in two-syllable words on the first syllable (*ama* /áma/ 'mother', *seme* /s'éme/ 'son') and in words with more syllables on the second: *gizona* /gisóna/ 'the man', *berria* /berría/ 'the new one', *autobusa* /awtóbus'a/ 'the bus'. These accent patterns can stretch over longer phrases in focal position (see lesson 1), with a prolonged flat or gradually descending pitch over the syllables following the one that carries the accent. In our transcription the stressed syllable is marked by an acute accent on the vowel or nuclear vowel in a diphthong: *eguna* /egúna/ 'the day', *gaua* /gáwa/ 'the night'.

EXERCISES

Exercise 1: Indicate the pronunciation including the stress of the following words, using the transcription explained above.

sagar, sagu, emakume, eder, gona, gorri, handi, txiki, mutil, jauna, euria, euskara, aita, hogei, goi, behi, tresna, argia, akerra, nagusia, zaldi, beltz, sorgina, apaiza, axola, hotz, atzo, ametsa, txar, txoria, bihotz.

Exercise 2: Deduce the correct spelling from the following transcriptions.

/s'énar/, /s'óka/, /ews'kálduna/, /úda/, /gérra/, /handítas'una/, /tshírla/, /bómbil/, /jáwntsho/, /elúrra/, /aytóna/, /hirúrogey/, /gáy/, /éhisa/, /ás'ko/, /has'érre/, /éltse/, /éltsho/, /soríona/, /hayséa/, /kútsha/, /útsi/, /jatétshe/, /sahárra/, /tshalóa/, /ahásti/.

LESSON **ONE**

LEHENENGO IKASGAIA

ELKARRIZKETA

Lehen elkarrizketa: Egun on!

Bernardo:	Egun on! Ni Bernardo naiz. Mutila naiz.
Jone:	Kaixo! Ni Jone naiz. Neska naiz.
Bernardo:	Nire izena Bernardo da. Ni Joneren neba naiz.
Jone:	Nire izena Jone da eta ni Bernardoren arreba naiz.
Bernardo:	Jone izen polita da. Zure izena polita da.
Jone:	Bai, polita da, baina Bernardo ere izen polita da.
Bernardo:	Oso pozik nago.
Jone:	Ikusi arte!

DIALOGUE

First conversation: Good morning!

Bernard: Good morning! I am Bernard. I am a boy.
Johanna: Hello! I am Johanna. I am a girl.
Bernard: My name is Bernard. I am Johanna's brother.
Johanna: My name is Johanna. I am Bernard's sister.
Bernard: Johanna is a nice name. Your name is nice.
Johanna: Yes, it is nice, but Bernard is a nice name too.
Bernard: I am very glad.
Johanna: See you!

VOCABULARY/HIZTEGIA

lehen	first
elkarrizketa	dialogue, conversation
egun/a	day
on	good
ni	I
mutil/a	boy
kaixo	hello, hi
neska	girl
nire	my
izen/a	name
neba	brother (of a female person)
eta	and
arreba	sister (of a male person)
polit	nice, pretty
zure	your (of one person)
bai	yes
baina	but
ere	too, also
oso	very
pozik	glad
ikusi	to see
arte	until

In the dialogue we encountered three expressions that are frequently used in conversations: the formal *Egun on!* (Good day! or, before lunch: Good morning!) and the informal *Kaixo!* (Hi! or Hello!), both used when people meet, and *Ikusi arte!* (See you! or Good-bye!), when people part. Here are a few more useful expressions:

EXPRESSIONS/ESAERAK

Agur!	Bye!, Good-bye!
Arratsalde on!	Good afternoon!, Good evening!
Gau on! (Gabon!)	Good night!
Gero arte!	See you later!
Hona hemen …	Here is, here are …
Laster arte!	See you soon!
Nire izena … da.	My name is …
Zure izena … da?	Is your name … ?

GRAMMAR

Nouns and noun phrases

A noun phrase consists of a noun accompanied by accessories such as qualitative or possessive adjectives. In the first dialogue we came across a few examples:

> *nire izena* my + name (a possessive and a noun)
> *izen polita* name + nice (a noun and an adjective)

The smallest possible noun phrase is a noun on its own, without any accessories:

> *neska* girl

The cases above show the order in which the different elements *must* be placed in a noun phrase: a possessive always precedes the noun, adjectives always come after the noun. As in English, a noun can be accompanied by a string of adjectives, but unlike in English, they all follow the noun. In practice, the number of adjectives that follow a noun is limited to two or three.

The definite article singular

In Basque there is no separate word that corresponds to the definite article 'the' in English. Instead, the ending *-a* is attached to the bare noun in order to make it definite:

> *egun* day > *eguna* the day
> *izen* name > *izena* the name

The same process can be applied to adjectives:

> *polit* nice > *polita* the nice one

We shall refer to the form without *-a* as the *indefinite* form of the noun or adjective. An indefinite noun in Basque is not necessarily the same as its English equivalent without article or preceded by 'a(n)'. *Egun* can mean 'a day' or 'day' or 'days' as the English convention would require in the applicable context. Should the indefinite already end in *-a*, then this final vowel is not reduplicated in the definite form, as shown by the example of the word *neska* (girl), which ends in *-a* and remains *neska* (the girl) in the definite form.

For all practical purposes, the ending *-a* can be called the equivalent of the definite article singular and the use of *-a* is very similar, though not identical, to that of 'the' in English. It is recommended to pay careful attention to the exercises to learn the correct application of the article in Basque.

In any noun phrase, even the most complex one, it is only the very last element that carries the marker *-a* to characterize the definiteness of the whole group:

izen name
*nire izen**a*** my name (the possessive comes first)
*izen polit**a*** the nice name (the adjective comes last)
*zure izen polit**a*** your nice name (possessive-noun-adjective)

All nouns in the vocabularies and in both glossaries of this book are shown in their indefinite form followed by a slash-*a* to illustrate the contrast between the definite and the indefinite. Where the slash-*a* is missing, the *a* is part of the noun itself:

izen/a name
neska girl

Since the concept of definite/indefinite typically relates to objects and living beings, i.e. to nouns, the slash-*a* convention is applied to nouns only, whereas adjectives are always shown like *polit* (nice) in their indefinite form.

The verb 'to be'

We distinguish two different forms of the verb 'to be'. The first one is *izan*, which is the copula (linking verb) used to express a permanent or inherent relationship between the subject and the predicate. We saw two applications of this in the dialogue, the conjugated forms *naiz* (am) and *da* (is):

(Ni Bernardo) naiz. (I) am (Bernard).
(Nire izena Bernardo) da. (My name) is (Bernard).

Izan is also used as the auxiliary verb in the intransitive conjugation. The full set of the present tense of *izan* is:

Izan	***To be***
Present tense	
Ni naiz	I am
Hi haiz	You (familiar) are
Zu zara	You (common singular) are
Hura da	He, she, it is
Gu gara	We are
Zuek zarete	You (plural) are
Haiek dira	They are

Notes on the table above:

1. The forms of the second person with *hi* (you) are typical of very familiar speech among close friends or relatives and will not be used in this book, except in the conjugation tables.

2. There is no reference to the sex of the third person: 'he', 'she', and 'it' are all referred to as *hura*.

Be careful in distributing the definite marker *-a* when the copula *izan* is used and note the difference between the following two sentences:

Izen polita da. It is a nice name.
Izena polita da. The name is nice.

The first sentence has its subject suppressed (see below under the topic 'The subject') and can also be read as *Hura izen polita da,* with the reinserted subject *Hura* (it). The predicate is the noun phrase *izen polita*, which requires just one *-a* at the very end. In the second sentence, however, the subject is explicit: *Izena* (the name) and the predicate is formed by *polita* (nice); both are definite and both require the marker *-a*.

The second option to render the English 'to be' is *egon*, which expresses a temporary state of the subject or its whereabouts. In the dialogue we met the first person singular *nago* (am) in Bernard answering that he is glad because Johanna says he has a nice name, not necessarily because he is happy by nature:

(Oso pozik) nago. (I) am (very glad).

The full set of the present tense of *egon* is:

Egon ***Present tense***	***To be***
Ni nago	I am
Hi hago	You (familiar) are
Zu zaude	You (common singular) are
Hura dago	He, she, it is
Gu gaude	We are
Zuek zaudete	You (plural) are
Haiek daude	They are

The subject

If there is no risk of misunderstanding and as long as the subject does not require any emphasis, it can be omitted:

> *Ni neska naiz.* Or: *Neska naiz.* I am a girl.
> *Zu mutila zara.* Or: *Mutila zara.* You are a boy.

Word order

If present, the subject usually precedes the conjugated form of the verb. But they can be separated by the predicate or the object (as we shall see later). In the following examples the so-called focal element *Bernardo* is inserted between the two:

> *Ni Bernardo naiz.* I am Bernard. (and not Peter!)
> *Nire izena Bernardo da.* My name is Bernard. (and not Peter!)

In the absence of an explicit subject the focal element remains in its place before the verb:

> *Mutila naiz.* I am a boy. (and not a girl!)

From the examples above it should be clear that the focal element or focus is that part of a sentence which contains new information or the part that answers a question (whether the question was explicitly asked or not). The focal slot in the sentence is the position just before the verb.

Questions

The simplest way of forming a question is by changing the rather flat intonation of a positive statement into a rise. Do not unnecessarily change the word order if you want to ask a question! *Nire izena Jone da* (My name is Johanna) is a simple statement which is turned into a question by the intonation, leaving the word order unchanged: *Zure izena Jone da?* (Is your name Johanna?).

ADDITIONAL VOCABULARY

andereño/a	young lady, Miss
andere/a	lady, Mrs.
Ane	Anna
emakume/a	woman
gizon/a	man (in general and/ or male person)
jaun/a	gentleman, Mr.
laster	soon, shortly
Mikel	Michael
nor	who

EXERCISES

Exercise 3: Translate into English.

1. Egun on! Ni mutila naiz.
2. Arratsalde on! Zu Bernardo zara?
3. Kaixo! Ni neska naiz.
4. Zu nor zara?
5. Ni Jone naiz.
6. Izen polita da.
7. Ni oso pozik nago. Gero arte!
8. Nor da hura? Ane da. Ane emakumea da.
9. Jone andereñoa da.
10. Eta zu nor zara? Ni Mikel naiz. Ni gizona naiz.
11. Zu pozik zaude.
12. Jauna oso pozik dago.

Exercise 4: Translate into Basque.

1. Hi! Is your name Maria?
2. Good afternoon, I am Maria.
3. Is Johanna a boy?
4. Johanna is a girl.
5. It is a nice day.
6. The day is nice.
7. Michael is my brother.
8. Anna is your sister.
9. Who is he? He is Bernard. He is a man.
10. And who is she? She is Johanna. She is a young lady.
11. She is very glad.
12. The lady is also glad.

LESSON**TWO**

BIGARRENIKASGAIA

ELKARRIZKETA

Nola duzu izena?

Bernardo: Nola duzu izena?
Miren: Nire izena Miren da.
Bernardo: Zu Joneren laguna zara?
Miren: Bai, ni Joneren laguna naiz.
Bernardo: Non dago Jone?
Miren: Jone ez dago hemen. Jone han dago.
Bernardo: Zu nola zaude?
Miren: Ondo nago, eskerrik asko! Eta zu?
Bernardo: Ni ez nago ondo. Gaixorik nago.
Jone: Egun on! Zer moduz zaudete?
Miren: Ni ondo nago, baina Bernardo ez dago ondo. Eta zu?
Jone: Ni oso ondo nago.
Miren: Hona hemen zure liburuak.
Jone: Non daude nire liburuak?
Miren: Begira: hemen dago liburu bat. Eta hona hemen beste liburu bat.
Jone: Eskerrik asko. Egiaz, nire liburuak dira. Bata zuria da eta bestea gorria.
Miren: Bihar arte!
Jone: Agur!

DIALOGUE

What is your name?

Bernard:	What is your name?
Maria:	My name is Maria.
Bernard:	Are you Johanna's friend?
Maria:	Yes, I am Johanna's friend.
Bernard:	Where is Johanna?
Maria:	Johanna is not here. Johanna is over there.
Bernard:	How are you?
Maria:	I am fine, thank you! And you?
Bernard:	I am not well. I am sick.
Johanna:	Good morning! How are you both?
Maria:	I am fine, but Bernard is not well. And you?
Johanna:	I am very well.
Maria:	Here are your books.
Johanna:	Where are my books?
Maria:	Look: here is one book. And here's another book.
Johanna:	Thanks a lot. These are indeed my books. One is white and the other one red.
Maria:	See you tomorrow!
Johanna:	Bye!

VOCABULARY/HIZTEGIA

nola	how
lagun/a	friend (boy or girl), companion
non	where
ez	no, not
hemen	here
han	there
ondo	well, fine
esker/ra	gratitude
asko	much, many
gaixorik	sick
zer	what
modu/a	way, manner
liburu/a	book
begiratu; begira!	to look; look!
bat	one, a(n)
beste	other
egia	truth
egiaz	truly, certainly, indeed
zuri	white
gorri	red
bihar	tomorrow

EXPRESSIONS/ESAERAK

Nola duzu izena?	What is your name? (lit.: "How do you have your name?")
Nola zaude?	How are you? (one person addressed)
Nola zaudete?	How are you? (more persons addressed)
Eskerrik asko!	Thanks a lot!
Ez horregatik!	You're welcome! (lit.: "Not because of that!")
Zer moduz zaude?	How are you? How are things? (one person addressed)
Zer moduz zaudete?	How are you? How are things? (more persons addressed)
Begira!	Look!
Bihar arte!	See you tomorrow!

GRAMMAR

The negation

'No' or 'not' is expressed by the particle *ez* placed in front of the verb:

Jone ez dago hemen. Johanna is not here.

The positive statement *Jone hemen dago* (Johanna is here) contains *hemen* as the focal element in front of the verb. The denial of this statement leaves the negation word *ez* in the focal slot of the sentence. Basque does not employ any of the auxiliary constructions like 'do not' and 'does not', which are characteristic of English, but simply inserts the negation marker *ez* in the sentence.

To be somewhere

The dialogue shows some cases of the application of the verb *egon* (to be) to indicate somebody's whereabouts (see the relevant remark under the second option for the verb 'to be' in lesson 1):

Non dago Jone? Where is Johanna?
Jone han dago. Johanna is over there.

Similarly with a plural subject:

Non daude liburuak? Where are the books?
Liburuak hemen daude. The books are here.

The strong r

When an indefinite form ends in *-r*, as is the case with the word *esker* (gratitude) in the dialogue, this is in most cases the so-called strong *r* /rr/ with the prolonged trill. To mark the correct pronunciation of the definite form with the attached *-a*, this *r* is reduplicated in the spelling:

esker (gratitude) > *eske**rr**a* (the gratitude)

In the vocabularies and the glossary you will find a slash between the two r's, indicating that one belongs to the noun as such and that the other one is its duplicate to preserve the correct pronunciation in the definite form: *esker/ra*. Note, however, that in normal writing, the rr-sequence which represents a single sound unit cannot be split.

The indefinite article

The English indefinite article 'a' or 'an' is in Basque *bat*, which is the same word as the numeral 'one'. It is placed after the noun it relates to and forms a single intonation unit with it:

book *liburu* /libúru/
the book *liburua* /libúrua/
a book *liburu bat* /libúrubat/

name *izen* /ísen/
the name *izena* /iséna/
a name *izen bat* /isémbat/

Note in the dialogue the definite occurrence of *bat* in the form of *bata*:

Bata zuria da. One is white. (i.e. the one in front of me, the first one, etc.)

The word beste *(other)*

The word 'other' in Basque is *beste*, which can take articles like any other noun or adjective: *bestea* (the other one), *beste bat* (another one). When 'another' is used as an attribute to a noun, then the noun must be preceded by *beste* and followed by *bat*:

another book *beste liburu bat*
another girl *beste neska bat*

not to be confused with:

the other book *beste liburua*
the other girl *beste neska*

which are definite and hence require the definite marker *-a* instead of the indefinite article *bat*. Unlike normal adjectives, *beste* always precedes the noun.

The plural article

In order to create the plural, the ending *-k* is added to the definite singular *-a*, forming *-ak* as the plural article. This plural marker is used with nouns and with adjectives ending a noun phrase or occurring in plural predicates. Remember that in noun phrases it is only the last element that carries the plural marker:

the book *liburu**a***
the books *liburu**ak***
the white books *liburu zuri**ak***
The books are white. *Liburu**ak** zuri**ak** dira.*

the girl *nesk**a***
the girls *nesk**ak***
the nice girls *neska polit**ak***
The girls are nice. *Nesk**ak** polit**ak** dira.*

The word batzuk *(some)*

The indefinite article *bat* can also be used in a plural form *batzuk* which means ‘some’ or ‘a few’:

liburu bat a book, one book
liburu batzuk some books

ADDITIONAL VOCABULARY

adiskide/a	friend
koaderno/a	notebook
nekaturik	tired
ordea	on the contrary

EXERCISES

Exercise 5: Translate into English.

1. Non dago Bernardo?
2. Bernardo han dago.
3. Hura nola dago?
4. Hura ondo dago.
5. Miren gaixorik dago.
6. Jone nekaturik dago.
7. Hona hemen mutil bat.
8. Liburua zuria da.
9. Beste liburua gorria da.
10. Koadernoa ere gorria da.
11. Hona hemen neska batzuk.
12. Izenak ez dira politak.
13. Neska nekaturik dago.
14. Bernardo ez da Joneren laguna: Joneren neba da.
15. Miren, ordea, Joneren laguna da.
16. Jone eta Miren lagunak dira.

Exercise 6: Translate into Basque.

1. Where are Bernard and Maria?
2. They are over there.
3. How are you (plural)?
4. We are fine.
5. Here is another boy.
6. Michael is my friend.
7. Anna is very tired.
8. My companion is sick.
9. The girls are very pretty.
10. Here are some books and notebooks.
11. The other book is not here.
12. Look, the white one is here!
13. Johanna is Bernard's sister.

14. Maria, on the contrary, is not Bernard's sister.
15. Maria is Johanna's friend.
16. They are friends.

Exercise 7: Complete the following answers.

Example: Zu Bernardo zara? Bai, ni Bernardo naiz.

1. Zu Jone zara? 1. Bai, ...
2. Zu mutila zara? 2. Ez, ...
3. Zure izena Bernardo da? 3. Bai, ...
4. Jone izen polita da? 4. Bai, ...
5. Miren neska polita da? 5. Bai, ...
6. Miren han dago? 6. Ez, ...
7. Haiek han daude? 7. Bai, ...
8. Hura nekaturik dago? 8. Ez, ...
9. Bernardo mutil ona da? 9. Bai, ...
10. Zu gaixorik zaude? 10. Ez, ...
11. Liburua zuria da? 11. Bai, ...
12. Liburuak han daude? 12. Ez, ...
13. Koadernoa gorria da? 13. Ez, ...
14. Ane zure laguna da? 14. Bai, ...
15. Zuek lagunak zarete? 15. Ez, gu ...
16. Mikel zure neba da? 16. Bai, ...

LESSON **THREE**

HIRUGARREN IKASGAIA

ELKARRIZKETA

Zu nongoa zara?

Pello:	Arratsalde on, Jone! Zu nongoa zara?
Jone:	Ongi etorri, Pello! Ni Euskal Herrikoa naiz. Ni euskalduna naiz.
Pello:	Ni, ordea, Ameriketakoa naiz. Ni amerikarra naiz.
Jone:	Zu Ameriketan bizi zara?
Pello:	Bai, ni Ameriketan bizi naiz. Eta zu, non bizi zara?
Jone:	Ni Bilbon bizi naiz. Noiz etorri zara Bilbora?
Pello:	Gaur etorri naiz. Hau nire lehen bisita da.
Jone:	Eta nola etorri zara? Abioiz ala trenez?
Pello:	Abioiz etorri naiz. Ez naiz trenez etorri.
Jone:	Abioia garaiz heldu da?
Pello:	Ez, abioia ez da garaiz heldu. Berandu heldu da.

DIALOGUE

Where are you from?

Peter:	Good afternoon, Johanna! Where are you from?
Johanna:	Welcome, Peter! I am from the Basque Country. I am Basque.
Peter:	I am from America. I am American.
Johanna:	Do you live in America?
Peter:	Yes, I live in America. And where do you live?
Johanna:	I live in Bilbao. When did you come to Bilbao?
Peter:	I came (lit.: have come) today. This is my first visit.
Johanna:	And how did you come? By plane or by train?
Peter:	I came (lit.: have come) by plane. I did not (lit.: have not) come by train.
Johanna:	Did the plane arrive on time?
Peter:	No, the plane did not arrive on time. It arrived late.

VOCABULARY

nongo	from where, originating
ongi	well
etorri	to come
Euskal Herri/a	the Basque Country
herri/a	land, country, place, village
euskaldun/a	Basque (speaking person)
Amerika	America
amerikar/ra	American
bizi izan	to live
Bilbo	(city of) Bilbao
noiz	when
gaur	today
hau	this
bisita	visit
abioi/a	airplane
egazkin/a	airplane
abioiz	by plane
ala	or
tren/a	train
trenez	by train
garaiz	in time
heldu	to arrive
berandu	late

In the dialogue we notice the welcoming expression *Ongi etorri!* (Welcome!). Some other useful expressions when meeting people are:

EXPRESSIONS/ESAERAK

Nongoa zara?	Where are you from?
Ongi etorri Euskal Herrira!	Welcome to the Basque Country!
Ongi etorri Ameriketara!	Welcome to America! (lit.: "to the Americas")
Ni Ameriketakoa naiz.	I am American. (lit.: "from the Americas")
Zu Euskal Herrikoa zara?	Are you Basque?
Non bizi zara?	Where do you live?
Bidaia on!	Have a good trip!
Ondo ibili!	Have a good trip! (lit.: "Walk well!")

GRAMMAR

The verb and its conjugation: General notions

In English dictionaries verbs are listed in the infinitive form such as '(to) be' and '(to) come'. Basque, on the contrary, lists them in the so-called *perfective* form, which is like the past participle in English. Hence, the form *etorri* in the vocabulary above really means '(have) come', just like *izan* and *egon* (see lesson 1) mean 'been'. Most verbs in Basque are only used in combination with some form of the auxiliary verbs 'to be' or 'to have'. In other words, even simple expressions like 'I go', 'you eat' and 'he worked' are usually rendered by forms like 'I am going', 'you are eating' and 'he has (had) worked'. The rule applies to all tenses and modes in the Basque conjugation. This conjugation is based on the required use of an auxiliary verb and will be referred to as the *complex* or *descriptive* conjugation. It is opposed to the *simple* or *synthetic* conjugation which applies to a very limited set of verbs only (see from lesson 7 onwards).

The perfective

Basque perfectives consist of a lexical root and a suffix that can be *-i*, *-tu*, or *-du*. Sometimes the root and the perfective are one and the same form. The following typical examples are given:

Perfective	*Meaning*	*Root*
etorri	come	etor
gertatu	happened	gerta
heldu	arrived	hel
igo	climbed	igo

The recent past tense

In this lesson we shall deal with intransitive verbs only, i.e. verbs which cannot be followed by a direct object. Many verbs of state or motion fall into this category. The dialogue above gives a number of examples of the *recent past tense* in Basque, which is formed by the perfective (past participle) in combination with the present tense of the auxiliary *izan* (see lesson 1). The recent past in Basque is translated in English by the simple past or perfect tense:

> *Gaur etorri naiz.* I came / have come today.
> *Abioia garaiz heldu da?* Did the plane arrive on time?

With words like *gaur* (today) and similar references to the present as viewed by the speaker, the recent past *must* be used in Basque. Note that in positive statements the main verb comes first and is followed by the auxiliary. The full set of the recent past in Basque is illustrated below using the verb *etorri* (to come):

Etorri ***Recent past tense***	***To come***
Ni etorri naiz	I came / have come
Hi etorri haiz	You (familiar) came / have come
Zu etorri zara	You (common singular) came / have come
Hura etorri da	He, she, it came / has come
Gu etorri gara	We came / have come
Zuek etorri zarete	You (plural) came / have come
Haiek etorri dira	They came / have come

The sequence main-auxiliary is inseparable: no elements can be placed between the two. In negative sentences the word order is inverted by placing the auxiliary in front of the main verb (only the translation in the perfect tense is given):

Ni ez naiz etorri	I have not come
Hi ez haiz etorri	You (familiar) have not come
Zu ez zara etorri	You (common singular) have not come
Hura ez da etorri	He, she, it has not come
Gu ez gara etorri	We have not come
Zuek ez zarete etorri	You (plural) have not come
Haiek ez dira etorri	They have not come

In this case additional elements may be placed between the auxiliary and the main. See for example *Ez naiz trenez etorri* (I have not come by train) in the dialogue above, where *trenez* (by train) is inserted.

The relational suffix -ko

Basque has a suffix *-ko* (*-go* after *n*) which is extensively used to express all sorts of relations of place, time, destination, and others. It can be attached to many categories of words. The derivate carries a meaning that can be inferred from the context. The following examples are given as illustrations of the use of this powerful suffix:

Bilbo Bilbao > *Bilbo**ko*** of, from, in Bilbao, Bilbao's
herri country > *herri**ko*** of the country, popular, 'folk'
gaur today > *gaur**ko*** today's, modern
non where > *non**go*** from where

Derivates ending in *-ko* are adjective type words, but they precede the noun when used as attributes:

gaurko liburua the modern book

When occurring as predicates they must be made definite in accordance with the rule explained in lesson 1:

*Liburua gaurko**a** da.* The book is modern.
*Ni Ameriketako**a** naiz.* I am from America.
*Mutila hemengo**a** da.* The boy is from here (is a local).
*Neskak hango**ak** dira.* The girls are from there.

The location suffix -n (geographical names)

Basque attaches the specific location suffix *-n* or *-en* to geographical names in order to express the meaning 'in that place'. Use *-n* with words that end with a vowel sound and *-en* with words that end with a consonant sound. The following examples illustrate this process:

Bilbo Bilbao > *Bilbo**n*** in Bilbao
Gernika Guernica > *Gernika**n*** in Guernica
Londres London > *Londres**en*** in London
New York New York > *New York**en*** in New York
Kalifornia California > *Kalifornia**n*** in California

The direction suffix -ra (geographical names)

The direction suffix *-ra* or *-era* is added to geographical names in order to express the meaning 'to that place'. The process works exactly the same way as with the location suffix *-n*:

Bilbo Bilbao > *Bilbo**ra*** to Bilbao
Gernika Guernica > *Gernika**ra*** to Guernica
Londres London > *Londres**era*** to London
New York New York > *New York**era*** to New York
Kalifornia California > *Kalifornia**ra*** to California

The word* ala *('or' exclusive)

In *Nola etorri zara? Abioiz ala trenez?* (How did you come? By plane or by train?) a choice must be made in the answer and one solution excludes the other. In such cases 'or' is translated by *ala*. Some other examples of questions where an exclusive answer may be expected, or is suggested, are:

Zu ala ni? You or I?
Gaur ala bihar? Today or tomorrow?
Lehen ala bigarren elkarrizketa? The first or the second dialogue?

ADDITIONAL VOCABULARY

Baiona	(city of) Bayonne
bigarren	second
Bilbo	(city of) Bilbao
Gernika	(city of) Guernica
Hegoalde/a	Southern Basque Country (in Spain), "the South"
hiri/a	city
hona	hither, here
Iparralde/a	Northern Basque Country (in France), "the North"
joan	to go

EXERCISES

Exercise 8: Translate into English.

1. Nongoa da mutila? Bilbokoa da.
2. Noiz etorri da Ameriketara? Gaur etorri da.
3. Non bizi dira neskak? Neskak Gernikan bizi dira.
4. Zu ere bizi zara Gernikan?
5. Ez, ni ez naiz Gernikan bizi. Ni Baionan bizi naiz.
6. Gernika Hegoaldean dago.
7. Baiona Iparraldean dago.
8. Noiz joan da trena Londresera? Trena gaur joan da.
9. Hau zure lehen bisita da? Ez, hau ez da nire lehen bisita.
10. Hau nire bigarren bidaia da.
11. Noiz heldu da abioia? Abioia ez da heldu.
12. Zuek Euskal Herrian ala Ameriketan bizi zarete?
13. Gu Ameriketan bizi gara; gu amerikarrak gara.
14. Non dago Bilbo?
15. Bilbo Hegoaldean dago.
16. Nongoak dira emakumeak? Emakumeak Iparraldekoak dira.

Exercise 9: Translate into Basque.

1. Where are the girls from? They are from Bayonne.
2. When did you (plural) come to Guernica? We arrived today.
3. Where does the man live? The man lives in the Northern Basque Country.
4. Do you (singular) also live in "the North"?
5. No, I live in "the South"; I live in Bilbao.
6. Guernica is a place in the Southern Basque Country.
7. Bayonne is a city in "the North."
8. When did the plane go to New York? The plane went today.

9. Is this your first or second trip?
10. This is my first visit.
11. Has the train arrived in Bilbao? No, it hasn't.
12. Have they come to California?
13. Yes, they are from California.
14. Where are you?
15. I am here; I came here.
16. Where are the boys from? They are from over there.

LESSON **FOUR**

LAUGARREN IKASGAIA

ELKARRIZKETA

Nondik nora?

Jone:	Aizu, Pello! Zer gertatu da? Gaixorik edo nekaturik al zaude?
Pello:	Sentitzen dut. Oraindik nekatu samar nago. Ni atzo iritsi nintzen Ameriketatik Euskal Herrira.
Jone:	Orduan, bidaia luzea zen. Hegaldia nekagarria al zen?
Pello:	Benetan, luzea zen. Azkenean oso nekaturik nengoen.
Jone:	Nondik nora joan zinen?
Pello:	Lehenik New Yorketik Londresera joan nintzen eta gero Londresetik Bilbora.
Jone:	Denbora luzean egon zinen Londresen?
Pello:	Ez, denbora gutxian bakarrik egon nintzen han.
Jone:	Orduan, bidaia luzea, baina atsegina zen.
Pello:	Arrazoi duzu, Jone. Lehen hegaldia luzea eta aspergarri samarra zen. Bigarren hegaldia, ordea, laburra eta interesgarria zen.

DIALOGUE

From where to where?

Johanna:	Listen, Peter! What has happened? Are you sick or tired?
Peter:	I am sorry. I am still rather tired. Yesterday I arrived from America in the Basque Country.
Johanna:	So it was a long trip. Was the flight tiring?
Peter:	It was really long. At the end I was very tired.
Johanna:	From where to where did you go?
Peter:	First I went from New York to London and then from London to Bilbao.
Johanna:	Did you spend much time in London?
Peter:	No, I was there only for a short while.
Johanna:	So it was a long but pleasant trip.
Peter:	You are right, Johanna. The first flight was long and rather boring. But the second flight was short and interesting.

VOCABULARY/HIZTEGIA

nondik	from where
nora	where to
edo	or
al	(interrogative particle—untranslated)
oraindik	still
samar	rather, somewhat
atzo	yesterday
iritsi	to arrive
orduan	then, so
luze	long
hegaldi/a	flight
nekagarri	fatiguing, tiring
benetan	truly, seriously, indeed
azkenean	at last, in the end
lehenik	first(ly), in the first place, before
denbora	time
denbora luzean	for a long time
denbora gutxian	for a short while
gutxi	little, few
bakarrik	only
atsegin	pleasant
aspergarri	boring
labur	short
interesgarri	interesting

EXPRESSIONS/ESAERAK

Aizu!	Listen!
Zer gertatu da?	What has happened?
Zer gertatzen da?	What's going on?
Sentitzen dut.	I am sorry.
Arrazoi duzu.	You are right.

GRAMMAR

The past tense of izan *(to be)*

The past tense of *izan* is used as a simple past or as part of the pluperfect tense, describing a state or action in a more remote past. The whole set is given first:

Izan	*To be*
Past tense	
Ni nintzen	I was
Hi hintzen	You (familiar) were
Zu zinen	You (common singular) were
Hura zen	He, she, it was
Gu ginen	We were
Zuek zineten	You (plural) were
Haiek ziren	They were

Statements that are valid in the present are converted to statements with a validity in the past just as in English:

Hegaldia luzea da. The flight is long.
Hegaldia luzea zen. The flight was long.

The remote past tense

The past tense of the auxiliary *izan* in combination with a perfective (past participle) forms the so-called *remote past tense* in Basque, translated in English by the simple past or pluperfect.

Atzo etorri nintzen. I came yesterday. Or: I had come yesterday.

With words like *atzo* (yesterday) and similar references to the past as viewed by the speaker, the remote past *must* be used in Basque.

The full set of the remote past is illustrated below using the verb *etorri* (to come):

Etorri	***To come***
Remote past tense	
Ni etorri nintzen	I came / had come
Hi etorri hintzen	You (familiar) came / had come
Zu etorri zinen	You (common singular) came / had come
Hura etorri zen	He, she, it came / had come
Gu etorri ginen	We came / had come
Zuek etorri zineten	You (plural) came / had come
Haiek etorri ziren	They came / had come

The past tense of egon *(to be)*

The simple past tense of 'to be' expressing a temporary state or the meaning of being somewhere is given in the table below:

Egon	***To be***
Past tense	
Ni nengoen	I was
Hi hengoen	You (familiar) were
Zu zeunden	You (common singular) were
Hura zegoen	He, she, it was
Gu geunden	We were
Zuek zeundeten	You (plural) were
Haiek zeuden	They were

The separation suffix -tik *(geographical names)*

The suffix *-tik* or *-etik* is employed to express separation, departure or removal from somewhere. It behaves exactly the same way as the suffixes *-n* (in a location) and *-ra* (to a location) which we met in lesson 3:

> *Donostia* San Sebastián > *Donostia***tik** (leaving / originating) from San Sebastián
> *Paris* Paris > *Paris***etik** from Paris
> *Filadelfia* Philadelphia > *Filadelfia***tik** from Philadelphia
> *Boston* Boston > *Boston***etik** from Boston

The interrogative particle al

A direct question to which a 'yes' or 'no' can be expected is characterized by a mere intonation rise at the end of the sentence (see lesson 1). Optionally the particle *al* is inserted before the copula or auxiliary: *Zure izena Jone da?* and *Zure izena Jone al da?* mean the same thing: 'Is your name Johanna?' Likewise: *Abioia garaiz heldu (al) da?* (Did the plane arrive on time?).

The word edo *('or' inclusive)*

Edo, like *ala*, means 'or', but questions with *edo* do not require an exclusive choice and allow answers like 'yes' or 'no' or even something totally different. See Johanna's question in the dialogue: *Gaixorik edo nekaturik al zaude?* (Are you sick or tired?). Both situations are possible and do not necessarily exclude each other. In fact, Peter's rather evasive answer was: *Sentitzen dut* (I am sorry).

Whereas *ala* can only occur in questions, *edo* can also appear in positive statements:

> *Bilbotik edo Donostiatik etorri zen.* He came from Bilbao or from San Sebastián (or perhaps even from somewhere else).

The word samar *(rather)*

The word *samar* can be added to an adjective or a qualitative adverb to weaken its impact. It is best translated as 'rather', 'somewhat', 'fairly' or similar adverbs:

> *Hegaldia luze samarra da.* The flight is rather long.
> *Berandu samar heldu da.* He arrived rather late.

When added to an adjective, the word *samar* takes over its article *-a* (and reduplicates its final *r*); with adverbs *samar* is invariant.

ADDITIONAL VOCABULARY

arratsaldean	in the afternoon
bide/a	road
Bizkaia	(province of) Vizcaya
Donostia	(city of) San Sebastián
eliza	church
etxe/a	house
geltoki/a	railway or bus station
goiz	early
goiz/a	morning
goizean	in the morning
handi	big, large
erdialde/a	city center
erdialdean	in the city center
gure	our
hor	there (near the addressed person)
ibili	to walk
ikusgarri	worth seeing
jaio	to be born
jatetxe/a	restaurant
Miarritze	Biarritz
txiki	small, little

EXERCISES

Exercise 10: Translate into English.

1. Non dago zure etxea? Nire etxea han dago.
2. Gure bidaia oso atsegina zen.
3. Nondik heldu zen trena? Trena Donostiatik heldu zen. Atzo goizean heldu zen.
4. Nora joan zen trena? Trena Miarritzera joan zen. Atzo arratsaldean joan zen.
5. Non dago Bilboko geltokia? Geltokia erdialdean dago.
6. Non daude Donostiako elizak? Donostiako elizak han daude.
7. Jatetxea oso handia da.
8. Euskal Herriko hiriak oso interesgarriak dira.
9. Atzo zer gertatu zen Gernikan?
10. Atzo ni ez nengoen Gernikan.
11. Non jaio zinen zu?
12. Ni Ameriketan jaio nintzen.
13. Liburua atsegina ala aspergarria da? Liburua atsegina da.
14. Gu hona ibili ginen; nekaturik geunden.
15. Nondik nora ibili zineten?
16. Donostiatik Gernikara ibili ginen.

Exercise 11: Translate into Basque.

1. Where is the restaurant? The restaurant is there (near you)!
2. My second visit was very pleasant.
3. Where did the plane come from? The plane arrived from Paris. It arrived yesterday.
4. Where did the plane go to? The plane went to London.
5. Where are you? We are in the city center.

6. Is the station there (near you)? Yes, it is here.
7. The church and the restaurant are over there.
8. The road here is very long; we are tired.
9. Is the city worth seeing? Yes, it is an interesting place.
10. What happened yesterday in San Sebastián?
11. Yesterday we were in Biarritz.
12. Was she born in the Northern Basque Country? No, she was born in "the South."
13. I went from "the North" to "the South"; it was an interesting journey.
14. Were you in Vizcaya?
15. No, I was not in Vizcaya; I spent little time in "the South."
16. Yesterday's long flight was boring.

LESSON**FIVE**

BOSTGARRENIKASGAIA

ELKARRIZKETA

Zu egarri zara?

Bernardo: Kaixo, Jone! Zer da hori?
Jone: Kaixo! Hau kikarakada bat kafe da. Kafe bat hartu dut.
Bernardo: Zuk ez duzu terik hartu?
Jone: Ez, nik ez dut terik hartu.
Bernardo: Nik, ordea, tea nahi dut. Ni egarri naiz. Nik zerbait edan nahi dut.
Jone: Ardorik edo urik nahi duzu?
Bernardo: Ez, hemengo ardoa ez da ona. Eta ez dut urik nahi, tea baizik.
Jone: Ez zara gose? Zer hartu duzu jateko?
Bernardo: Ez, ni ez naiz gose. Nik ez dut ezer hartu.
Jone: Kafea oso ona da. Nik beste kikarakada bat nahi dut. Eta jan nahi dut. Ni gose naiz.
Bernardo: Hemengo pastelak goxoak dira. Pastelik nahi duzu?
Jone: Bai, pastel zati bat nahi dut. Zati handi bat nahi dut.
Bernardo: Zati hau hartu nahi duzu?
Jone: Bai, zati hori nahi dut. Eskerrik asko!

DIALOGUE

Are you thirsty?

Bernard: Hi, Johanna! What is that?
Johanna: Hi! This is a cup of coffee. I'm having (lit.: have taken) a coffee.
Bernard: Aren't you having (lit.: haven't you taken) tea?
Johanna: No, I'm not having (lit.: I haven't taken) tea.
Bernard: But I want tea. I am thirsty. I want to drink something.
Johanna: Do you want wine or water?
Bernard: No, the wine here is not good. And I don't want water, but tea.
Johanna: Aren't you hungry? What have you had (lit.: taken) to eat?
Bernard: No, I am not hungry. I haven't had (lit.: taken) anything.
Johanna: The coffee is very good. I want another cup. And I want to eat. I am hungry.
Bernard: The cakes here are sweet. You want some cake?
Johanna: Yes, I want a piece of cake. I want a big piece.
Bernard: You want to take this piece?
Johanna: Yes, I want that piece. Thanks a lot!

VOCABULARY/HIZTEGIA

egarri izan	to be thirsty
hori	that (near the listener)
kikara	(small) cup
kikarakada	a cup full of …
kafe/a	coffee
hartu	to take
te/a	tea
nahi ukan (izan)	to want
zerbait	something
edan	to drink
ardo/a	wine
ur/a	water
baizik	but, however
gose izan	to be hungry
ezer	anything (in negations)
jan	to eat
pastel/a	cake
goxo	sweet
zati/a	piece, part

EXPRESSIONS/ESAERAK

Zer da hori?	What's that?
Zer da gauza hori?	What's that thing?
Ni egarri naiz.	I'm thirsty.
Ni gose naiz.	I'm hungry.
Zer dago edateko?	What is there to drink?
Nik … edan nahi dut.	I want to drink …
Nik … nahi dut edateko.	I want … for a drink.
Zer dago jateko?	What is there to eat?
Nik … jan nahi dut.	I want to eat …
Nik … nahi dut jateko.	I want … for food.

GRAMMAR

The verb 'to have'

The verb *ukan* means 'to have'. It is used as an autonomous verb with the meaning 'to possess' and as the auxiliary of the transitive conjugation. The present tense and the past tense of *ukan* are given in the two following tables:

Ukan	***To have***
Present tense	
Nik dut	I have
Hik duk / dun	You (familiar, male / female) have
Zuk duzu	You (common singular) have
Hark du	He, she, it has
Guk dugu	We have
Zuek duzue	You (plural) have
Haiek dute	They have

Ukan	***To have***
Past tense	
Nik nuen	I had
Hik huen	You (familiar) had
Zuk zenuen	You (common singular) had
Hark zuen	He, she, it had
Guk genuen	We had
Zuek zenuten	You (plural) had
Haiek zuten	They had

The transitive subject

In Basque, subjects of transitive phrases take the ending *-k* (or *-ek* following a consonant or a diphthong in *-u*). Note the different form of the third person singular as a transitive subject: *hark* in lieu of the intransitive *hura*. It is essential to become familiar with the basic distinction between transitive and intransitive conjugations and subjects as illustrated by the few examples below:

Intransitive		*Transitive*	
Ni Bernardo naiz.	I am Bernard.	**Nik tea dut.**	I have tea.
Zu Jone zara.	You are Johanna.	**Zuk kikara duzu.**	You have the cup.
Miren etorri da.	Maria has come.	**Mirenek pastela du.**	Maria has the cake.

The transitive *-k* after the definite singular *-a* yields the form *-ak*, which is not to be confused with the intransitive plural:

		Transitive singular	
Mutilak ura du.	The boy has water.	**Mutilak etorri dira.**	The boys have come.

The transitive plural is distinguished from the transitive singular in that the former changes from *-ak* to *-ek*:

		Transitive singular	
Mutilak ura du.	The boy has water.	**Mutilek ura dute.**	The boys have water.

Note that it is the transitive subject that takes a case ending (*-k* or *-ek*) and *not* the direct object as people familiar with the accusative case in German, Russian or Latin might be tempted to think! The case which corresponds to the transitive subject is called the *ergative* case, and is one of the most characteristic features of Basque.

The transitive conjugation

Unlike English, which uses the single auxiliary 'to have' to express complex time relations, Basque adopts the intransitive *izan* with intransitive verbs like *etorri* (to come), but the transitive *ukan* in combination with transitive verbs like *nahi* (to want) or *edan* (to drink).

The perfective *ukan* is often substituted by *izan*, sometimes with the word 'transitive' added in brackets. In dictionary entries and in running text it is therefore not uncommon to encounter forms like *nahi izan* instead of *nahi ukan*. Note, however, that in transitive applications only the transitive conjugation can be used: *Nik ura dut* (I have water), *Zuk edan nahi duzu* (You want to drink), and also *Hark etorri nahi du* (He wants to come), etc. The widespread usage of *izan* is reflected in this grammar by adding *izan* in brackets to *ukan*.

The recent past and remote past tense (transitive)

As in the intransitive conjugation the recent past tense is formed by the perfective followed by the present tense of the auxiliary, this time *ukan*. As an example of the recent past tense in the transitive conjugation, the verb *edan* (to drink) is chosen. The full set is:

Edan	***To drink***
Recent past tense	
Nik (ardoa) edan dut	I drank / have drunk (the wine)
Hik (ardoa) edan duk / dun	You (familiar, male / female) drank / have drunk (the wine)
Zuk (ardoa) edan duzu	You (common singular) drank / have drunk (the wine)
Hark (ardoa) edan du	He, she, it drank / has drunk (the wine)
Guk (ardoa) edan dugu	We drank / have drunk (the wine)
Zuek (ardoa) edan duzue	You (plural) drank / have drunk (the wine)
Haiek (ardoa) edan dute	They drank / have drunk (the wine)

The remote past tense is created by the perfective followed by the past tense of *ukan*:

Edan	***To drink***
Remote past tense	
Nik (ardoa) edan nuen	I drank / had drunk (the wine)
Hik (ardoa) edan huen	You (familiar) drank / had drunk (the wine)
Zuk (ardoa) edan zenuen	You (common singular) drank / had drunk (the wine)
Hark (ardoa) edan zuen	He, she, it drank / had drunk (the wine)
Guk (ardoa) edan genuen	We drank / had drunk (the wine)
Zuek (ardoa) edan zenuten	You (plural) drank / had drunk (the wine)
Haiek (ardoa) edan zuten	They drank / had drunk (the wine)

The rules for application of the recent past versus the remote past tense are the same as in the intransitive conjugation. Also, no element can be placed between the main verb (*edan* in the case above) and the auxiliary. In the elaborate examples above, the object *ardoa* (the wine) has been located before the verbal complex to underline its focal role in the sentence: *Zuk ardoa edan duzu, baina nik ura* (You have drunk wine, but I (have drunk) water). Again, following the example of the intransitive conjugation, the word order is inverted in negative sentences, and other elements can then be placed between the auxiliary and the main verb:

Affirmative	*Negative*
Jonek ardoa edan du.	**Jonek ez du ardoa edan.**
Johanna has drunk the wine.	Johanna has not drunk the wine.

Plural objects

When a transitive verb has a plural object, the conjugated form of *ukan* shows this by inserting *-it-* before the root vowel *-u-*. To illustrate this in all clarity, the conjugation of *edan* (to drink) in both past tenses is fully repeated, but with the plural object *ardoak* (the wines):

Edan	*To drink*
Recent past tense (plural object)	
Nik (garagardoak) edan ditut	I drank / have drunk (the beers)
Hik (garagardoak) edan dituk / ditun	You (familiar, male / female) drank / have drunk (the beers)
Zuk (garagardoak) edan dituzu	You (common singular) drank/have drunk (the beers)
Hark (garagardoak) edan ditu	He, she, it drank / has drunk (the beers)
Guk (garagardoak) edan ditugu	We drank / have drunk (the beers)
Zuek (garagardoak) edan dituzue	You (plural) drank / have drunk (the beers)
Haiek (garagardoak) edan dituzte*	They drank / have drunk (the beers)

Edan	***To drink***
Remote past tense (plural object)	
Nik (garagardoak) edan nituen	I drank / had drunk (the beers)
Hik (garagardoak) edan hituen	You (familiar) drank / had drunk (the beers)
Zuk (garagardoak) edan zenituen	You (common singular) drank/ had drunk (the beers)
Hark (garagardoak) edan zituen	He, she, it drank / had drunk (the beers)
Guk (garagardoak) edan genituen	We drank / had drunk (the beers)
Zuek (garagardoak) edan zenituzten*	You (plural) drank / had drunk (the beers)
Haiek (garagardoak) edan zituzten*	They drank / had drunk (the beers)

Note that the theoretical sequence *-itute* in the cases marked with * is changed into *-ituzte*!

The singular/plural variation in the conjugated forms of *ukan* is of course also applicable in those cases where *ukan* is used as an autonomous verb with the meaning 'to have' or 'to possess':

Zuk ardoa duzu / zenuen. You have / had the wine.
*Zuk pastelak d**it**uzu / zen**it**uen.* You have / had the cakes.

The partitive suffix -(r)ik

When a noun occurs in a negative or interrogative sentence and it concerns something indefinite, e.g. an unstated quantity, the so-called partitive suffix *-ik* (after consonants) or *-rik* (after vowels) is attached to the bare noun.

*Nik ardo**a** hartu dut.* I have taken the wine. (affirmative)
*Nik ez dut ardo**a** hartu.* I haven't taken the wine. (negative, but definite)
*Nik ez dut ardo**rik** hartu.* I haven't taken any wine. (negative and indefinite)

Hark kafe **bat** *nahi du.* She wants a coffee. (affirmative)
*Hark ez du kafe**rik** nahi.* She doesn't want any coffee. (negative and indefinite)

*Zuk pastel**a** jan duzu.* You have eaten the cake. (affirmative)
*Zuk pastel**ik** nahi duzu?* Do you want any cake(s)? (interrogative and indefinite)

The partitive is interpreted as a singular form and consequently the last example above shows the form *duzu* and not *dituzu*. For the same reason we have *dago* and not *daude* in the following intransitive case:

Ez dago mutilik. There is no boy. Or: There aren't any boys.

Is/Are there (any) ...?

To translate the common question 'Is/Are there (any) ...?' we use the expression *Badago ...?* or, including the interrogative particle: *Ba al dago ...?* Here, *dago* is the known third person singular form of the verb *egon* including the new prefix *ba-*, which focalizes the verb, i.e. the being or not being there of the item we ask for. The subject of such questions obviously requires the partitive case:

Is there (any) wine? *Badago ardo**rik**?* or: *Ba al dago ardo**rik**?*
Are there (any) cakes? *Badago pastel**ik**?* or: *Ba al dago pastel**ik**?*

The word baizik *(but)*

Instead of *baina* (but) the word *baizik* is commonly used to express the contrary of a preceding negative statement. In the dialogue we saw the example *Ez dut urik nahi, tea baizik* (I don't want water, but tea). Similarly: *Ez bat, asko baizik* (Not one, but many). The word *baizik* is usually placed at the very end of the "corrective" statement.

ADDITIONAL VOCABULARY

bero	warm, hot
edalontzi/a	(drinking) glass
esne/a	milk
garagardo/a	beer
hotz	cold
hutsik	empty
katilu/a	bowl
nolako	what kind of
ogi/a	bread

EXERCISES

Exercise 12: Translate into English.

1. Ni gose naiz. Nik pastel zati bat jan nahi dut.
2. Miren egarri zen. Mirenek ura edan nahi zuen.
3. Zuek kaferik hartu duzue?
4. Ez, guk ez dugu kaferik hartu.
5. Zuk kikara ikusi al zenuen?
6. Bai, nik kikara ikusi nuen.
7. Ez, nik ez nuen kikara ikusi; nik ez nuen kikararik ikusi.
8. Zer da gauza hori? Hau kikarakada bat kafe da.
9. Eta zer da beste gauza hori?
10. Ez dut ezer ikusi.
11. Pastel batzuk jan nahi ditut eta esnea edan nahi dut.
12. Haiek pastelak hartu zituzten.
13. Guk liburu bat hartu nahi dugu.
14. Hark ardo asko edan zuen.
15. Nik edontzi edo katilu batzuk hartu nituen.
16. Zuek mutilak ikusi dituzue.
17. Zuk ura edan al duzu?
18. Bai, nik ura edan dut; ur hotza edan dut.
19. Ez, nik ez dut urik edan.
20. Ni ez naiz egarri izan; edontzia hutsik dago.
21. Badago esnerik?
22. Ba al dago libururik?

Exercise 13: Translate into Basque.

1. We are thirsty. We want to drink water.
2. Bernard was hungry. Bernard wanted to eat a few cakes.
3. Have they taken any tea?
4. Yes, they have taken tea.

5. Had he seen any friends?
6. No, he had not seen any friends or companions.
7. The boys and the girls had gone.
8. What is that? Is that water or white wine?
9. I did not see anything.
10. He wanted milk for a drink.
11. You (plural) are hungry; do you want any bread for food?
12. We had taken the bread.
13. She wanted to take one notebook.
14. Yesterday we drank a lot of wine.
15. I have seen the glasses, the cups and the bowls.
16. I wanted to take the book.
17. Did you see the girls?
18. Yes, I saw them.
19. No, I did not see any girls.
20. I was not hungry yesterday; I did not eat anything.
21. Is there any water?
22. Are there cups?

LESSON**SIX**

SEIGARRENIKASGAIA

DIALOGUE

Bazkaria prest dago.

Jone: Etorri hona, Bernardo! Jatordua da. Bazkaria prest dago. Ez al duzu ikusten?

Bernardo: Ikusten dut. Tira! Mahai hori beterik dago.

Jone: Mahai hau nik prestatu dut. Mahaian daude platerak, sardeskak, koilarak eta aiztoak.

Bernardo: Plater horiek ikusten ditut, sardeskak eta koilarak ere bai, baina ez ditut aiztoak ikusten. Barkatu, baina, ez dut aiztorik ikusten!

Jone: Etorri mahaira, aiztoak hemen daude.

Bernardo: Gaur zer dago jateko? Oraindik ez dut ezer ikusten.

Jone: Lehenik sarrerak daude eta gero haragia eta barazkiak.

Bernardo: Eta zer dago edateko?

Jone: Ura ekarri dut. Gaur goizean ardoa eta sagardoa erosi ditut. Hauek ere mahaian daude.

Bernardo: Ardo zuririk erosi al duzu?

Jone: Ez, ez dut zuririk erosi. Beltza bakarrik erosi dut. Bi botila erosi ditut.

Bernardo: Ez ditut botila horiek ikusten. Ardo botila bat bakarrik ikusten dut.

Jone: Botila bat mahaian dago, bestea sukaldean utzi dut.

DIALOGUE

Lunch is ready.

Johanna: Come over here, Bernard! It is time to eat. Lunch is ready. Don't you see?

Bernard: I see. Look at that! The table is full.

Johanna: I have prepared this table. There are dishes, forks, spoons and knives on the table.

Bernard: I see the dishes and the forks and spoons too, but I don't see the knives. Sorry, but I don't see any knives!

Johanna: Come to the table, the knives are here.

Bernard: What is there to eat today? I don't see anything yet.

Johanna: First there are appetizers and afterwards meat and vegetables.

Bernard: And what is there to drink?

Johanna: I have brought water. This morning I have bought wine and cider. They are also on the table.

Bernard: Have you bought any white wine?

Johanna: No, I haven't bought any white wine. I have only bought red. I have bought two bottles.

Bernard: I don't see those bottles. I see only one wine bottle.

Johanna: There is one bottle on the table, the other one I have left in the kitchen.

VOCABULARY

bazkari/a	lunch
prest	ready
jatordu/a	lunchtime, dinnertime
mahai/a	table
beterik	full
prestatu	to prepare
mahaian	on the table
plater/a	dish
sardeska	fork
koilara	spoon
aizto/a	knife
ere bai	too, as well (in truncated expressions)
ere ez	neither, not either (in truncated expressions)
oraindik ez	not yet
sarrera	appetizers
haragi/a	meat
barazki/a	vegetable
ekarri	to bring
sagardo/a	cider
erosi	to buy
beltz	black, red (dark red wine color)
bi	two
botila	bottle
sukalde/a	kitchen
sukaldean	in the kitchen
utzi	to leave

EXPRESSIONS/ESAERAK

Etorri hona!	Come here!
Tira!	Look at that!, Wow!
Barkatu!	Excuse me!, Sorry!

GRAMMAR

The imperfective

The imperfective of a Basque verb, comparable to the present participle in English, is formed by adding the ending *-ten* or *-tzen* to the verbal root in accordance with the following rules:

1. Roots of perfectives ending in *-n* replace the *-n* with *-ten*:
   izan been > *izaten* being
   joan gone > *joaten* going
   jan eaten > *jaten* eating
   edan drunk > *edaten* drinking

2. Roots ending in an affricate followed by *-i* reduce the affricate to the equivalent friction sound (e.g. *ts*>*s*, etc.) and replace *-i* with *-ten*:
   iritsi arrived > *iristen* arriving
   jantzi dressed > *janzten* dressing
   erakutsi showed > *erakusten* showing
   utzi left > *uzten* leaving

3. All other roots take *-tzen*:
   etorri come > *etortzen* coming
   ibili walked > *ibiltzen* walking
   gertatu happened > *gertatzen* happening
   heldu arrived > *heltzen* arriving
   igo climbed > *igotzen* climbing
   ikusi seen > *ikusten* seeing
   ekarri brought > *ekartzen* bringing

The (habitual) present and past tense

The (habitual) present tense of intransitive verbs is created by combining the imperfective with the appropriate form of the present tense of the auxiliary *izan* (to be):

Etorri	***To come***
(Habitual) present tense	
Ni etortzen naiz	I come
Hi etortzen haiz	You (familiar) come
Zu etortzen zara	You (common singular) come
Hura etortzen da	He, she, it comes
Gu etortzen gara	We come
Zuek etortzen zarete	You (plural) come
Haiek etortzen dira	They come

The (habitual) past tense of intransitive verbs is created by combining the imperfective with the appropriate form of the past tense of the auxiliary *izan* (to be):

Etorri	***To come***
(Habitual) past tense	
Ni etortzen nintzen	I came / used to come
Hi etortzen hintzen	You (familiar) came / used to come
Zu etortzen zinen	You (common singular) came / used to come
Hura etortzen zen	He, she, it came / used to come
Gu etortzen ginen	We came / used to come
Zuek etortzen zineten	You (plural) came / used to come
Haiek etortzen ziren	They came / used to come

Following exactly the same process, the habitual present and past tense of transitive verbs is created by combining the imperfective with the appropriate form of the present or past tense of the auxiliary *ukan* (to have):

Edan	***To drink***
(Habitual) present tense (singular object)	
Nik edaten dut	I drink (it)
Hik edaten duk / dun	You (familiar, male / female) drink (it)
Zuk edaten duzu	You (common singular) drink (it)
Hark edaten du	He, she, it drinks (it)
Guk edaten dugu	We drink (it)
Zuek edaten duzue	You (plural) drink (it)
Haiek edaten dute	They drink (it)

Edan	***To drink***
(Habitual) past tense (singular object)	
Nik edaten nuen	I drank / used to drink (it)
Hik edaten huen	You (familiar) drank / used to drink (it)
Zuk edaten zenuen	You (common singular) drank / used to drink (it)
Hark edaten zuen	He, she, it drank / used to drink (it)
Guk edaten genuen	We drank / used to drink (it)
Zuek edaten zenuten	You (plural) drank / used to drink (it)
Haiek edaten zuten	They drank / used to drink (it)

The sample conjugation above has been simplified a bit because by now the reader will have acquired some familiarity with the impact of singular/plural objects on the form of the conjugated verb. The following examples with plural objects should be self-explanatory, because the well known infix *-it-* turns up again (see lesson 5).

> *Nik ardo zuriak edaten **nit**uen.* I used to drink white wines.
> *Zuk liburuak erosten d**it**uzu.* You are buying the books.

The demonstrative pronouns

As was the case with the location adverbs *hemen* (here, near the speaker), *hor* (there, near the listener), and *han* (there, away from the speaker and the listener) that we have seen already, Basque also distinguishes three degrees of proximity in the demonstrative pronouns:

Demonstrative pronouns

Singular	***Plural***
hau this (near the speaker)	**hauek** these (near the speaker)
hori that (near the listener)	**horiek** those (near the listener)
hura that (near others)	**haiek** those (near others)

A demonstrative pronoun can be used to specify a noun, in which case it follows the noun like any attributive adjective:

> *Liburu hau interesgarria da.* This book is interesting.
> *Etxe hori handia da.* That house (of yours) is big.
> *Botila hura txikia da.* That bottle (over there) is small.

Or, in the plural:

> *Ardo hauek onak dira.* These wines are good.
> *Pastel horiek goxoak dira.* Those cakes (next to you) are sweet.
> *Mahai haiek handiak dira.* Those tables (over there) are big.

In the presence of adjectives, the demonstrative pronoun comes at the very end of the noun phrase:

pastel goxo hau this sweet cake
etxe txiki hori that small house
mahai handi hura that big table

Demonstrative pronouns can also be used autonomously, as subjects or objects in their own right, as the following examples illustrate:

Hau nire liburua da. This is my book.
Hori zure etxea da. That is your house.
Hura Joneren kafea da. That is Johanna's coffee.

Or, in the plural:

Hauek ardo onak dira. These are good wines.
Horiek liburu aspergarriak dira. Those are boring books.
Haiek pastel goxoak dira. Those are sweet cakes.

Note that *hura* and *haiek* are also used as personal pronouns of the third person, as we saw earlier in the different conjugations: *hura da* (he, she, it is), *haiek etorri dira* (they have come), etc. It is quite normal to use a demonstrative pronoun in Basque where in English the article would suffice, as a few examples in the dialogue demonstrated.

Adverbs of state

In the sentence *Mahai hori beterik dago* (The table is full) the predicate 'full' is not translated by the adjective *bete*, but by the derived form *beterik*. We call this an *adverb of state* and predicates of this kind indicate a temporary state or situation. The corresponding verb is often *egon*, as we remember from lesson 1. The underlying "literal" meaning of *Mahai hori beterik dago* is "The table shows itself as being full" or something of the kind. From the previous lessons we remember:

Gaixorik nago. I am sick. < *gaixo* sick, e.g. *mutil gaixoa* the sick boy
Edontzia hutsik dago. The glass is empty. < *huts* empty, e.g. *edontzi hutsa* the empty glass

Returning to the fundamental difference between *izan* and *egon*: statements including *izan* correspond to questions with *nolakoa(k)* (how, what kind of); those including forms of *egon* imply questions with *nola* (how) or *non* (where). Compare:

Mahaia beterik dago. The table is full.
Mahaia handia da. The table is big.

The latter one corresponds to the question *Nolakoa da mahaia?* (What kind of table is it?).

Clearly, it is the suffix *-ik* (after consonants) or *-rik* (after vowels) which turns a true qualifying adjective into an adverb of state. This process, however, is not productive (it does not automatically apply to any adjective), and there is no simple rule to distinguish adjectives which allow this formation from those that don't. A short list of adjectives which allow the derivation with *-(r)ik* is given below together with their corresponding adverbs of state:

bizi alive, lively > *bizirik* (being) alive
erotu gone mad > *eroturik* madly, in a state of madness
gazte young > *gazterik* in one's youth
isil silent > *isilik* silently, secretly
nekatu tired > *nekaturik* in a state of fatigue
oso complete, total > *osorik* completely, totally
zahar old > *zaharrik* in one's old age

ADDITIONAL VOCABULARY

afari/a	dinner, late evening meal
askotan	often, many times
beti	always
edari/a	drink
garagardo/a	beer
gosari/a	breakfast
janari/a	food
lehen	before

EXERCISES

Exercise 14: Translate into English.

1. Zuek haragirik hartzen duzue?
2. Ez, guk ez dugu haragirik hartzen.
3. Zuk botila ikusten al duzu?
4. Bai, nik botila ikusten dut.
5. Ez, nik ez dut botila ikusten; nik ez dut botilarik ikusten.
6. Zer da gauza hori? Hau botila bat ardo da. Ardo beltza da.
7. Eta zer da beste gauza hori?
8. Ez dut ezer ikusten.
9. Haiek platerak ekartzen dituzte.
10. Guk sardeskak eta aiztoak hartzen ditugu.
11. Hark ardo asko edaten du; lehen ardo gutxi edaten zuen.
12. Nik barazki asko jaten ditut.
13. Sukaldean garagardoa eta sagardoa daude; han ez dago ardorik.
14. Nolako ardoa da hori?
15. Hau beltza da; hura ez da beltza; zuria da.
16. Mahaian garagardoa dago.
17. Garagardo hura ona al da?
18. Oso ona da benetan.
19. Zer gertatzen da han?
20. Ez da ezer gertatzen han.
21. Haiek beti trenez joaten ziren Baionara.
22. Zu askotan etortzen zinen hona.

Exercise 15: Translate into Basque.

1. Does he take any milk?
2. No, he does not take any milk; he takes appetizers.
3. Do they see the plates on the table?
4. Yes, they see the plates.

5. However, I do not see the plates; I do not see anything.
6. What did she bring? She brought the forks, the spoons and the knives.
7. And what is that?
8. This is cider; we bought it this morning.
9. The wine we bought yesterday.
10. They used to eat much meat.
11. They do not eat any meat today.
12. Do you always eat vegetables?
13. We often drink beer or milk.
14. Hi! Is that white wine?
15. Good afternoon! No, this is water.
16. The wine is still in the kitchen.
17. What is that over there?
18. Those are the appetizers; Maria prepared them this morning.
19. What was it he used to buy?
20. He used to buy lots of books.
21. We used to come here many times.
22. They always go to San Sebastián by train.

LESSON **SEVEN**

ZAZPIGARREN IKASGAIA

ELKARRIZKETA

Zenbat lore?

Jone: Egun on, Bernardo! Zenbat urte ditu Mirenek?

Bernardo: Kaixo! Berak hamasei urte ditu, nik bezala. Gaur bere jaioteguna da. Loreak erosi behar ditugu.

Jone: Arrazoi duzu, baina ez dut dirurik. Zuk baduzu dirurik? Nahikoa da?

Bernardo: Itxaron... Bat, bi, hiru, lau... bost euro ditut sakelan. Nire ustez nahikoak dira.

Jone: Goazen loreak erostera! Han loradenda dago.

Saltzailea: Egun on! Zer nahi duzue? Lorerik erosi nahi duzue, edo landarerik?

Bernardo: Baduzu arrosarik? Lore fresko eta ederrak erosi nahi ditugu. Zenbat balio dute arrosek, mesedez?

Saltzailea: Arrosak garestiak dira. Hauek bost euro, haiek garestiagoak dira: zazpi euro balio dute.

Jone: Beti merkeak erosten ditugu. Bost euro bakarrik dauzkagu.

Saltzailea: Merkeak ere oso ederrak dira. Eta oso freskoak ere bai. Hauek hartu nahi dituzue? Tori! Zerbait gehiago?

Bernardo: Ez, hori da dena. Eskerrik asko. Tori, bost euroko bilete bat. Ikusi arte!

Jone: Sentitzen dut, Bernardo... Ez dut ondo bilatu... Nik ere bilete batzuk dauzkat sakelan. Begira: hiru bilete eta txanpon bi aurkitu ditut.

Bernardo: Ez du axola. Arrosa hauek ederrak dira. Goazen Mirenen etxera!

DIALOGUE

How many flowers?

Johanna: Good morning, Bernard! How old is Maria?

Bernard: Hi! She is sixteen years old, just like me. Today is her birthday. We must buy flowers.

Johanna: You are right, but I have no money. Do you have any money? Is it enough?

Bernard: Wait… One, two, three, four… five euros I have in my pocket. I think they are enough.

Johanna: Let's go and buy flowers! Over there is a florist's shop.

Salesperson: Good morning! What do you want? Do you want to buy any flowers, or a plant?

Bernard: Do you have roses? We want to buy fresh and nice flowers. How much are the roses, please?

Salesperson: The roses are expensive. These are five euros, those over there are more expensive: they cost seven euros.

Johanna: We always buy the cheap ones. We only have five euros.

Salesperson: The cheap ones are also very nice. And very fresh as well. Do you want to take these? Here you are! Anything else?

Bernard: No, that is all. Thank you. Here you are, a five euro note. See you!

Johanna: I am sorry, Bernard… I haven't searched well… I have a few banknotes in my pocket as well. Look: I have found three notes and two coins.

Bernard: It doesn't matter. These roses are beautiful. Let's go to Maria's home!

VOCABULARY/HIZTEGIA

zenbat	how much, how many
lore/a	flower
urte/a	year
bera	he, she, it
bezala	just like, as
bere	his, her, its
jaiotegun/a	birthday
behar ukan (izan)	to have to
diru/a	money
nahiko	enough, sufficient
sakela	pocket
sakelan	in the pocket
loradenda	florist (store)
saltzaile/a	salesperson
landare/a	plant
arrosa	rose
fresko	fresh
eder	beautiful
balio ukan	to cost, to be worth
garesti	expensive
merke	cheap
gehiago	more
den/a	everything, all
bilete/a	banknote
bilatu	to look for, to search
txanpon/a	coin
aurkitu	to find
etxera	home (directional)

EXPRESSIONS/ESAERAK

Itxaron!	Wait!
Nire (Zure) ustez.	In my (your) view.
Goazen!	Let's go!
Goazen … erostera!	Let's go and buy …!
Goazen … jatera (edatera)!	Let's go and eat (drink) …!
Zenbat balio du (dute) …?	How much is (are) …?
Nahikoa da … erosteko?	Is it enough to buy …?
Mesedez!	Please!
Tori!	Here you are, there you are!
Zerbait gehiago?	Anything else?
Hori da dena.	That's all.
Ez du axola.	It does not matter.

GRAMMAR

Numerals/Zenbakiak (1–20)	
The basic cardinal numbers in Basque are:	
bat	one
bi	two
hiru	three
lau	four
bost	five
sei	six
zazpi	seven
zortzi	eight
bederatzi	nine
hamar	ten
hamaika	eleven
hamabi	twelve
hamahiru	thirteen
hamalau	fourteen
hamabost	fifteen
hamasei	sixteen
hamazazpi	seventeen
hamazortzi	eighteen
hemeretzi	nineteen
hogei	twenty

Note the indefinite form of the noun following *zenbat* (how much, how many) in *zenbat* ***lore*** (how many flowers) and pay attention to the use of the verbs in questions with *zenbat*:

Zenbat esne dago sukaldean? How much milk is there in the kitchen?
Zenbat botila daude mahaian? How many bottles are there on the table?

In the first sentence the singular *dago* is used, because the question concerns the collective noun 'milk' and an answer like 'much', 'little' or 'none' is expected. The second sentence, however, shows the plural *daude*, and this is because *botila* is a numerable noun and we rather expect a discrete number as a reply: 'two', 'three', etc. Hence the question in the dialogue *Zenbat urte ditu Mirenek?* (How old is Maria?, literally: "How many years does Maria have?"), with the plural object marker *-it-* inserted: ***ditu***.

All cardinal numbers precede the noun or noun phrase they refer to, except for *bat* (see also lesson 1). The number *bi* (two) can be placed before or after the noun:

zenbat lore? how many flowers?
lore bat one flower
lore eder bat one beautiful flower
lore bi, bi lore two flowers
hiru lore three flowers
lau lore four flowers
etc.

Once again the fine distinction between the indefinite and definite forms of the noun is emphasized:

bost lore five flowers
*bost lore***ak** the five flowers
bost lore eder five beautiful flowers
*bost lore eder***rak** the five beautiful flowers

A number higher than one does not by itself require the following noun (phrase) to be put in the plural: the plurality is given by the presence of the numeral. Only if the noun (phrase) is meant to be *definite*, the ending *-ak* is added.

Do you have (any) ...?

The question 'Do you have (any) ...?' is translated as *Baduzu ... (r)ik?* in a way comparable to what we saw in lesson 5 under the header 'Is/Are there (any) ...?' The same prefix *ba-* is added to the already known *duzu* to focalize the verb, in this case the having or not having of the item we are after:

Do you have (any) money? *Baduzu dirurik?*
Do you have (any) roses? *Baduzu arrosarik?*

The words bera(k) *and* bere(n) *(third persons)*

When the English 'he', 'she', or 'it' refers to a person or a topic that has just been mentioned, the form *bera* (lit.: "the same one") is used in lieu of *hura*. The corresponding possessive is *bere* (his, her, its, lit.: "of the same one"):

Zenbat urte ditu Mirenek? Berak hamasei urte ditu. Gaur bere jaioteguna da. How old is Maria? She is sixteen years old. Today is her birthday.
Non dago Bernardo? Hona hemen bere liburua. Where's Bernard? Here is his book.

In all other cases where another or an unrelated person or topic appears, the already known *hura* applies, with its corresponding possessive *haren* (of the other one): *haren liburua* 'his (her) book', *haren loreak* 'his (her) flowers'.

The same reasoning applies to the third person plural, where *haiek* (they) is replaced by *berak* as long as no new topic is introduced; the corresponding possessive is *beren* (their).

The verbs 'to want to' and 'to have to'

Nahi ukan (izan) (lesson 5) means 'to want (to)', 'to desire' and *behar ukan (izan)* 'to have to' or 'to need'. The conjugation shows up in the different forms of *ukan*, including, where needed, the plural insert. If 'to want to' or 'to have to' is followed by a verb (I want to buy something, I have to read a book), this verb appears in its perfective form in the focal position just before *behar* or *nahi*, as illustrated below:

Loreak ***erosi*** *behar ditugu.* We must buy flowers.
Nik liburu hau ***irakurri*** *behar dut.* I must read this book.
Zuk pastel horiek ***jan*** *nahi dituzu.* You want to eat those cakes.
Lorerik ***erosi*** *nahi duzue?* Do you want to buy any flowers?

Note that the partitive required in the interrogative sentence is seen by the verb as a singular form, hence *duzue* in the last sentence and not *dituzue*.

The comparative

The comparative (cheap > cheaper, expensive > more expensive) is rendered in Basque by the suffix *-ago* added to the adjective or the adverb:

garesti > *garesti**ago*** expensive > more expensive
luze > *luze**ago*** long > longer
labur > *labur**rago*** (with the final *r* reduplicated!) short > shorter

Comparative adjectives are, of course, declined like any other adjective:

*Lore hau merkea da, hori merke**agoa** da.* This flower is cheap, that one is cheaper.
*Liburu hauek ederrak ziren, haiek eder**ragoak**.* These books were nice, those (were) nicer.

The verb eduki (to hold)

The transitive verb *eduki* (to hold) is used as a substitute for *ukan* (to have) meaning 'to possess, to hold'. It is frequently used in the so-called simple conjugation, i.e. without any auxiliary. Like all transitive verbs, it distinguishes between a singular and plural object. In the dialogue we saw the sentence *Bost euro bakarrik dauzkagu* (We only have five euros) with the plural object *Bost euro* requiring the plural insert *-z-* in *dauzkagu* 'we have (them)'. In the following illustration the object is either *liburua* (the book) or *liburuak* (the books).

Eduki	***To hold***
Simple present tense (singular object)	
Nik liburua daukat	I have the book
Hik liburua daukak / daukan	You (familiar, male / female) have the book
Zuk liburua daukazu	You (common singular) have the book
Hark liburua dauka	He, she, it has the book
Guk liburua daukagu	We have the book
Zuek liburua daukazue	You (plural) have the book
Haiek liburua daukate	They have the book

Eduki	***To hold***
Simple present tense (plural object)	
Nik liburuak dauzkat	I have the books
Hik liburuak dauzkak / dauzkan	You (familiar, male / female) have the books
Zuk liburuak dauzkazu	You (common singular) have the books
Hark liburuak dauzka	He, she, it has the books
Guk liburuak dauzkagu	We have the books
Zuek liburuak dauzkazue	You (plural) have the books
Haiek liburuak dauzkate	They have the books

The above listed forms are almost synonymous to forms derived from *ukan* (to have): *Nik liburua(k) dut (ditut)*, 'I have the book(s)', *Hark liburua(k) du (ditu)*, 'He has the book(s)', but they evoke more the idea of physically holding something in the hand, possessing something, than the weaker forms of *ukan*. Note that the plural object marker is an inserted -*z*- *(daukat* > *dau***z***kat)* and not the -*it*- of *ukan (dut* > *d***it***ut)*.

ADDITIONAL VOCABULARY

aberats	rich
behartsu	poor
itsusi	ugly
saldu	to sell

EXERCISES

Exercise 16: Translate into English.

1. Hark zenbat diru behar du? Hogei euro behar ditu.
2. Diru asko behar du; ez da gizon aberatsa.
3. Loreak ez dira garestiak; arrosa ederrak erosi ditugu.
4. Ikusi al duzu Miren?
5. Berak loreak saltzen ditu. Han bere loradenda dago.
6. Landare hori ez da merkea.
7. Ez dugu erosi landarerik: lore haiek merkeagoak dira.
8. Zenbat euro dauzkazu sakelan?
9. Nik hamar euro dauzkat: hamar euroko bilete bat daukat sakelan.
10. Zer saltzen dute? Loreak saltzen dituzte.
11. Diru hau nahikoa da loreak erosteko?
12. Bai, diru hori nahikoa da.
13. Tori, bilete bi eta txanpon batzuk!
14. Arrosa horiek erosi nahi ditugu: ederrak eta oso freskoak dira. Ez dira itsusiak.
15. Saltzaileak lore freskoak saltzen zituen; bere arrosak oso ederrak ziren.
16. Dirua nire sakelan bilatu behar dut; ez dut bileterik edo txanponik aurkitu.
17. Baduzu dirurik sakelan?
18. Baduzu platerik sukaldean?

Exercise 17: Translate into Basque.

1. Do you have any money in your pocket? I do not have any money.
2. I need little money: I am not a poor man.
3. Flowers and plants are cheap here; we want to buy seventeen roses.
4. Do you see Johanna over there? She is the salesperson!

5. They used to sell books and notebooks.
6. That wine (of yours) is not cheap, but very expensive: it costs twelve euros.
7. We used to buy nothing.
8. Do you have any five euro notes in your pocket?
9. Yes, there you are! But I only have one five euro note.
10. Does she indeed sell books?
11. One ten euro note is enough to buy this bottle of wine.
12. It is not enough to buy that beautiful book over there.
13. Look! Here is a twenty euro note and also some coins.
14. I want to buy these small notebooks.
15. He used to buy big houses.
16. I am, however, looking for a nice, small house.
17. Do you have any flowers?
18. Do you have coins in your pocket?

LESSON **EIGHT**

ZORTZIGARREN IKASGAIA

ELKARRIZKETA

Astearen egunak.

Miren:	Gaur astelehena da. Astelehena astearen lehen eguna da.
Bernardo:	Bai, horixe da! Astelehena ez da egun berezia, laneguna baizik.
Jone:	Baina gaurko eguna benetan berezia da: Mirenen jaioteguna da.
Miren:	Gaur ez naiz eskolara joango. Bihar itzuliko naiz eskolara. Bihar asteartea izango da.
Bernardo:	Asteak zazpi egun ditu eta asteartea bigarrena da.
Jone:	Etzi asteazkena izango da; asteazkena hirugarren eguna da.
Miren:	Orduan inor ez da eskolara joango. Aurten jaieguna izango da. Iaz ez zen jaieguna izan.
Bernardo:	Beste bi lanegunak osteguna eta ostirala dira. Gero asteburua izango da.
Jone:	Larunbatean eta igandean libre egongo gara. Igandea astearen azken eguna da: zazpigarren eguna da.

DIALOGUE

The days of the week.

Maria: Today is Monday. Monday is the first day of the week.

Bernard: Yes, precisely! Monday is not a special day, but a working day.

Johanna: But today is truly special: it is Maria's birthday.

Maria: Today I am not going to school. Tomorrow I shall return to school. Tomorrow will be Tuesday.

Bernard: A week has seven days and Tuesday is the second one.

Johanna: The day after tomorrow will be Wednesday; Wednesday is the third day.

Maria: Nobody will then go to school. It will be a holiday this year. Last year it was not a holiday.

Bernard: The other two working days are Thursday and Friday. Then there will be the weekend.

Johanna: Saturday and Sunday we shall be free. Sunday is the last day of the week: it is the seventh day.

VOCABULARY/HIZTEGIA

aste/a	week
astelehen/a	Monday
berezi	special
lanegun/a	working day
eskola	school
eskolara	to school
itzuli	to return, to go back
astearte/a	Tuesday
etzi	the day after tomorrow
asteazken/a	Wednesday
hirugarren	third
inor	anybody (in negations)
aurten	this year
jaiegun/a	holiday
iaz	last year
ostegun/a	Thursday
ostiral/a	Friday
asteburu/a	weekend
larunbat/a	Saturday
larunbatean	on Saturday
igande/a	Sunday
igandean	on Sunday
libre	free
azken	last, final

EXPRESSIONS/ESAERAK

Horixe da!	Precisely! Exactly! Just like you said!
Aulki hori libre dago?	Is that chair free?

GRAMMAR

The future tense

The future participle is formed by adding the ending *-ko* (*-go* after a final *n*) to the perfective of the verb. Its approximate meaning is 'about to …' or 'to be …-ing':

> *etorri* come > *etorri**ko*** about to come, to be coming
> *joan* gone > *joan**go*** about to go, to be going
> *irakurri* read > *irakurri**ko*** about to read, to be reading

The future tense is formed by combining the future participle with the appropriate form of the present tense of one of the auxiliary verbs *izan* or *ukan*, as in the example from the dialogue: *Bihar itzuliko naiz eskolara* (Tomorrow I shall go back to school). The following two tables give complete sets of the transitive and intransitive future, which differ by the use of the auxiliary and by the characteristic transitive form of the subject:

Joan	***To go***
Future tense (intransitive)	
Ni (eskolara) joango naiz	I shall go (to school)
Hi (eskolara) joango haiz	You (familiar) will go (to school)
Zu (eskolara) joango zara	You (common singular) will go (to school)
Hura (eskolara) joango da	He, she, it will go (to school)
Gu (eskolara) joango gara	We shall go (to school)
Zuek (eskolara) joango zarete	You (plural) will go (to school)
Haiek (eskolara) joango dira	They will go (to school)

Irakurri	***To read***
Future tense (transitive, singular object)	
Nik (liburua) irakurriko dut	I shall read (the book)
Hik (liburua) irakurriko duk / dun	You (familiar, male / female) will read (the book)
Zuk (liburua) irakurriko duzu	You (common singular) will read (the book)
Hark (liburua) irakurriko du	He, she, it will read (the book)
Guk (liburua) irakurriko dugu	We shall read (the book)
Zuek (liburua) irakurriko duzue	You (plural) will read (the book)
Haiek (liburua) irakurriko dute	They will read (the book)

It goes without saying that the plural insert *-it-* makes its appearance as soon as a plural object is used:

Nik liburuak irakurriko ditut. I shall read the books.

Numerals (ordinal numbers)

The ordinal numbers (second, third, etc.) are derived from the cardinals (two, three, etc.) by adding the suffix *-garren* to them. This is an absolutely regular process, with the exception of the very first ordinal 'first', which we already met as *lehen*. Note the small spelling adaptation in 'fifth': the final *t* of *bost* 'five' is dropped in the pronunciation of *bosgarren* /bos'kárren/:

bat one > *lehen* first
bi two > *bigarren* second
hiru three > *hirugarren* third
lau four > *laugarren* fourth
bost five > *bosgarren* fifth
etc.

Like cardinal numbers, ordinals also precede the noun (phrase). This applies as well to *azken* (last): *azken aguna* (the last day). They can also be used autonomously or as predicates, i.e. as definite forms with the added *-a*:

> *bigarren eguna* the second day
> *bigarren**a*** the second one, number two
> *Elkarrizketa hau bigarren**a** da.* This dialogue is the second one.
> *Azken**a** iritsi da.* The last one has arrived.

The genitive suffix -ren

The suffix *-ren* combined with the definite singular of a noun yields the genitive case of this noun and expresses a relation of inherent interdependence between two items, e.g. between 'day' and 'week' in 'the days of the week':

> *aste**a*** the week > *aste**aren*** of the week > *aste**aren** egunak* the days of the week

This is in contrast with the relational suffix *-ko* (lesson 3), which expresses a less intrinsic, perhaps even casual or temporary relationship, though often rendered by the preposition 'of' in English. Remember also that *-ko* comes after the indefinite of the noun. The difference between *-ren* and *-ko* should be evident in the two sample cases (*atea* is 'the door' and *giltza* means 'the key'):

> *ate**aren** giltza* the key of/to the door, i.e. that particular key that belongs to the door
> *ate**ko** giltza* the key of/in the door, i.e. the key that happens to be in the lock

With names of living beings *-ren* is the only suffix allowed to express a genitive:

*mutil**aren** izena* the boy's name
*emakume**aren** loreak* the woman's flowers

This includes proper names, which are definite by definition so that the *-ren* (or *-en* after consonants) attaches directly to the name:

*Jon**eren** liburuak* Johanna's books (in lesson 2's dialogue)
*Miren**en** jaioteguna* Maria's birthday (in this lesson's dialogue)

ADDITIONAL VOCABULARY

ate/a	door
giltz/a	key
hil/a	month
hilabete/a	(whole) month
lan/a	work, task
lan egin	to work
urtaro/a	season

EXERCISES

Exercise 18: Translate into English.

1. Zenbat egun ditu asteak? Asteak zazpi egun ditu.
2. Zenbat aste ditu hilabeteak? Lau aste.
3. Urteak lau urtaro ditu.
4. Atzo oso berandu etorri zineten etxera, beti bezala.
5. Gu beti berandu etortzen gara etxera.
6. Gaur goizean garaiz etorri gara etxera.
7. Bihar ere garaiz etorriko gara.
8. Osteguna astearen laugarren eguna da. Beti bezala lan egiten dugu.
9. Bihar ere lan egingo dugu. Ostirala izango da, bosgarren eguna.
10. Etzi ez dugu egingo lan. Asteburua izango da eta libre egongo gara.
11. Laneguna ez da egun berezia.
12. Igandea egun berezia da: libre egoten gara.
13. Gaur hilaren lehen eguna da, baina bihar urtearen azken eguna izango da.
14. Etzi, ordea, urtearen lehen eguna izango da.
15. Urtearen lehena jaieguna izaten da.
16. Oraindik ez dut irakurri liburu hau; bihar irakurriko dut.

Exercise 19: Translate into Basque.

1. Does a week have five days? No, a week has five working days.
2. There are four weeks in a month (the month's weeks are four).
3. This is the year's first season.
4. Last year we bought beautiful flowers.
5. We used to buy flowers often (lit.: many times).
6. This afternoon we bought flowers and plants.
7. Tomorrow we shall not buy anything.

8. Monday is the first day of the week.
9. Tomorrow will be Tuesday; it will be a working day, like today.
10. Yesterday was Sunday, a special day.
11. Sunday is the second day of the weekend; the first one is Saturday.
12. The boy goes to school: it is not a holiday today.
13. The house has three doors and only one door has a key.
14. I am looking for the key of (to) the door.
15. Where was the key?
16. The key was in the kitchen.

LESSON**NINE**

BEDERATZIGARRENIKASGAIA

ELKARRIZKETA

Hirian.

Jone: Gaur ikusiko dugu nire hiria. Badakizunez, ni hirian bizi naiz.

Pello: Atseginez! Ni gustura joango naiz.

Jone: Entzun: hemen dago nire etxea, kale handi, zabal batean. Kale hau geltokitik ibaira doa.

Pello: Bai, ikusten dut. Eta beste etorbide hori, nondik nora doa?

Jone: Etorbide hau ibaiaren beste ertzean dago eta zubitik mendira doa. Goazen!

Pello: Hemen datoz Bernardo eta Miren.

Bernardo: Kaixo, Pello! Ikusten al duzu etxe handi hura? Hiriko antzokia da. Berria da: hiru urte bakarrik ditu.

Miren: Eta urruti beste teatro bat dago; zaharragoa da, baina oraindik erabiltzen dute.

Pello: Zer da leku hau? Non gaude eta gero nora goaz?

Jone: Leku hau enparantza da eta bere erdian oroitarri bat dago. Eskuinera eta ezkerrera arkuak daude. Hemen erdialde zaharrean gaude; oraintxe hemendik beste ertzera goaz eta hango jatetxe batean bazkalduko dugu.

Pello: Pilotalekura ere joango gara?

Jone: Bai, baina hara ez gara oinez joango, autobusez baizik. Gure pilotalekua ez dago hurbil, urruti baizik.

Pello: Hemendik urruti, bai, baina nire hoteleko auzoan dago. Han denok afalduko dugu elkarrekin!

DIALOGUE

In the city.

Johanna: Today we shall visit my city. I live in the city, as you know.

Peter: With pleasure! I shall be pleased to go.

Johanna: Listen: here is my house, in a big, broad street. This street goes from the station to the river.

Peter: Yes, I see. And that other avenue, from where to where does it go?

Johanna: This avenue lies on the other side of the river and goes from the bridge to the mountains. Let's go!

Peter: Here come Bernard and Maria.

Bernard: Hi, Peter! Do you see that big building? It is the city theater. It is new: it is only three years old.

Maria: And in the distance is another theater; it is older, but they still use it.

Peter: What is this place? Where are we and where shall we go later?

Johanna: This place is the square and in the middle of it stands a monument. To the right and to the left are arches. We are here in the old city center; right now we go from here to the other riverside and there we shall have lunch in a restaurant.

Peter: Shall we also go to the jai alai court?

Johanna: Yes, but we shall not go there walking but by bus. Our jai alai court is not nearby, but far away.

Peter: Far from here, but it is in the area of my hotel. There we shall have dinner all together!

VOCABULARY/HIZTEGIA

gustura	gladly, with pleasure
kale/a	street
zabal	broad, wide
ibai/a	river
etorbide/a	avenue
ertz/a	bank, riverside
zubi/a	bridge
mendi/a	mountain(s)*
antzoki/a	theater
berri	new
urruti	far away
teatro/a	theater
erabili	to use
leku/a	place
enparantza	city square
erdi/a	middle, half
oroitarri/a	monument, statue
eskuin/a	right-hand side
ezker/ra	left-hand side
arku/a	arch
oraintxe	right now
bazkaldu	to lunch
pilotaleku/a	jai alai court
hara	there, to that place
oin/a	foot
oinez	on foot, walking
autobus/a	bus
autobusez	by bus
hurbil	nearby
hotel/a	hotel
auzo/a	area, district
denok	all of us, all of you, all of them
afaldu	to dine
elkarrekin	together

**mendi* often carries the plural or collective meaning of 'mountains' in English, comparable to *montagne* in French.

EXPRESSIONS/ESAERAK

Badakizunez.	As you (singular) know.
Atseginez.	With pleasure.
Entzun!	Listen!
... eskuinera dago.	To the right there is ...
... ezkerrera dago.	To the left there is ...

GRAMMAR

The simple conjugation:* etorri *(to come) and* joan *(to go)
As was stated in lesson 7, a number of verbs have a *simple* conjugation in addition to the *descriptive* one. In the simple conjugation it is the main verb itself that undergoes certain changes to reflect the different tenses and modes, without the use of the auxiliaries *izan* or *ukan*. The verb *eduki* (to hold) was our first, transitive example. The dialogue above shows a few instances of the important verbs of motion *etorri* (to come) and *joan* (to go). The full sets of the simple present tense of these verbs are:

Etorri	***To come***
Simple present tense	
Ni nator	I come
Hi hator	You (familiar) come
Zu zatoz	You (common singular) come
Hura dator	He, she, it comes
Gu gatoz	We come
Zuek zatozte	You (plural) come
Haiek datoz	They come

Joan	***To go***
Simple present tense	
Ni noa	I go
Hi hoa	You (familiar) go
Zu zoaz	You (common singular) go
Hura doa	He, she, it goes
Gu goaz	We go
Zuek zoazte	You (plural) go
Haiek doaz	They go

In those cases where a verb has both a descriptive and a simple conjugation, the simple present is the unmarked tense, whereas the complex present expresses the habitual aspect. Note the difference between the two forms:

Ni nator. I come, I am coming. (simple present)
Ni etortzen naiz. I come, I have the habit of coming. (habitual present)
Hura doa. She goes, she is going. (simple present)
Hura joaten da. She goes, she has the habit of going. (habitual present)

If a verb can only be conjugated the complex way, i.e. using an auxiliary, then the epithet 'habitual' does not necessarily apply, which explains the use of the brackets around the word 'habitual' whenever the descriptive present was explained:

Trena heltzen da. The train is arriving (arrives now).
Trena garaiz heltzen da beti. The train always arrives on time.

The location suffix -an

The suffix *-an* (*-ean* after consonants) is attached to common noun phrases in their indefinite form to yield the meaning 'in that place' (compare *-n* for geographical names in lesson 3):

etxe house > *etxe**an*** in the house, at home
ertz riverside > *ertz**ean*** on the riverside

etxe handi big house > *etxe handi**an*** in the big house
kale zabal broad street > *kale zabal**ean*** in the broad street
jatetxe bat a restaurant > *jatetxe bat**ean*** in a restaurant

If a noun ends in *-a*, this is not reduplicated (the *-a* of the suffix is dropped and only *-n* is used):

eliza church > *eliza**n*** in the church

***The direction suffix* -ra**

The suffix *-ra* (*-era* after consonants) is attached to common noun phrases in their indefinite form to yield the meaning 'to that place' (compare *-ra* for geographical names in lesson 3):

etxe house > *etxe**ra*** to the house, home
leku bat a place > *leku bat**era*** to a place

***The separation suffix* -tik**

The suffix *-tik* (*-etik* after consonants) is attached to common noun phrases in their indefinite form to yield the meaning 'leaving or originating from that place' (compare *-tik* for geographical names in lesson 4):

etxe house > *etxe**tik*** from the house
leku bat a place > *leku bat**etik*** from a place

ADDITIONAL VOCABULARY

atze/a	the back
aurre/a	the front
barru/a	the inside
inguru/a	the surroundings
itsaso/a	sea
kanpo/a	the outside
mendialde/a	countryside, in the mountains

EXERCISES

Exercise 20: Translate into English.

1. Atzo ikusi nuen zure herria.
2. Herri hura mendialdean dago.
3. Hoteletik antzokira goaz.
4. Denok teatroan geunden.
5. Teatroaren barrua oso ederra da, kanpoa, ordea, itsusia.
6. Hiriaren inguruan mendiak daude.
7. Bihar hiritik mendira igoko dira.
8. Ibaia menditik itsasora doa.
9. Zuek zubian zaudete eta erdialdea ikusten duzue.
10. Oraintxe enparantzara goaz eta arkuak ikusiko ditugu.
11. Elizaren aurrea eskuinera dago.
12. Ezkerrera geltoki zaharraren atzea zegoen.
13. Etxetik pilotalekura beti oinez joaten gara: ibiltzen gara.
14. Urruti mendiak ikusten ditut.
15. Etzi joango naiz hara.
16. Itsasoa ez dago oso hurbil.

Exercise 21: Translate into Basque.

1. The day after tomorrow we all shall visit Bayonne.
2. The city lies on the bank of the river.
3. They come from the house to the station.
4. He was at the jai alai court.
5. The surroundings of the village are beautiful.
6. In the distance you see the sea.
7. Today we go to the mountain(s).
8. You will all have lunch together.
9. I was in the city square and saw the monument.
10. The avenue is very broad.

11. To the left is my house; to the right there is the church.
12. We shall walk from the church to the bridge.
13. We always go by bus to the sea.
14. Your hotel is nearby.
15. Last year they had dinner at the hotel.
16. We live in the old house in the countryside.

LESSON**TEN**

HAMARGARRENIKASGAIA

ELKARRIZKETA

Goazen geltokira!

Pello: Bihar beste herri batera joango naiz. Bertan hotel bat behar dut, baina ez dut inor ezagutzen.

Bernardo: Lasai, Pello! Jadanik aurkitu dut gela oso eder bat. Dirudienez, oso handia eta erosoa da. Bigarren oinean dago. Gelak dutxa, telefonoa, eta telebista ditu.

Pello: Jadanik erreserbatu al duzu gela hori?

Bernardo: Bai, telefonoz erreserbatu nuen. Bihar eguerdian gela prest egongo da.

Pello: Eskerrik asko! Orain nora joan nahi duzu? Nora goaz?

Bernardo: Orain geltokira goaz. Hara ez gara autobusez joango, oinez baizik, hurbil baitago. Zure txartela erosi behar dugu.

Pello: Zein leihatila da gurea?

Bernardo: Lehena da gurea, nazioartekoa da.

Pello: Zoritxarrez! Ikusten al duzu? Leihatilaraino ilara luzea dago. Denbora luzean itxaron behar dugu.

Bernardo: Ez gabiltza presaka. Ordu erdi barru ilararen bururaino iritsiko gara. Bitartean gure euskarazko elkarrizketa jarraituko dugu.

Pello: Konforme, beti euskaraz mintzatu behar dugu. Euskaraz mintzatuko gara!

DIALOGUE

Let's go to the station!

Peter: Tomorrow I shall go to another place. I need a hotel there, but I don't know anybody.

Bernard: Take it easy, Peter! I have already found a very nice room. As it seems, it is very big and comfortable. It is on the second floor. The room has a shower, telephone, and television.

Peter: Have you booked that room yet?

Bernard: Yes, I booked it by telephone. Tomorrow at noon the room will be ready.

Peter: Thanks a lot! Where do you want to go now? Where do we go?

Bernard: Now we go to the station. We shall not go there by bus, but walking, since it is nearby. We must buy your ticket.

Peter: Which counter is ours?

Bernard: The first one is ours, it is the international one.

Peter: Bad luck! Do you see? There is a long line at (lit.: until) the counter. We have to wait a long time.

Bernard: We are not in a hurry. Within half an hour we shall get to the front (lit.: end) of the line. In the meantime we shall continue our conversation in Basque.

Peter: Agreed, we must speak Basque all the time. We shall speak Basque!

VOCABULARY/HIZTEGIA

bertan	there, in that same place
ezagutu	to know
lasai egon	to be comfortable, to feel at ease
jadanik	already, yet
gela	room
eroso	comfortable
oin/a	floor
dutxa	shower (bath)
telefono/a	telephone
telebista	television
erreserbatu	to book, to reserve
telefonoz	by phone
eguerdi/a	noon
eguerdian	at noon
txartel/a	ticket
zein	which
leihatila	box-office window, counter
nazioarteko	international
ilara	line, row
itxaron	to wait
presaka	hurried, in a hurry
presaka ibili	to be in a hurry
ordu/a	hour
barru	within
buru/a	head, extremity, end
bitartean	meanwhile, in the meantime
euskara	Basque language
euskarazko	Basque (adjective)
jarraitu	to continue, to follow
mintzatu	to speak (intransitive!)

EXPRESSIONS/ESAERAK

Ezagutzen al duzu ...?	Do you know ...?
Bai, ezagutzen dut.	Yes, I know him/her.
Ez, ez dut ezagutzen.	No, I don't know him/her.
Lasai!	Easy!, Take it easy!
Oso lasai nago.	I really feel at ease.
Dirudienez ...	It seems that ...
... hurbil baitago.	... because it is nearby.
... urruti baitago.	... because it is far away.
Zoritxarrez!	Bad luck! What a pity!
Zorionez!	Fortunately!
Presaka nabil.	I am in a hurry.
Zu presaka zabiltza?	Are you in a hurry?
Konforme.	I agree. It's ok with me.

GRAMMAR

Ibili *(to walk) in the simple conjugation*

The third important verb of motion, after *etorri* (to come) and *joan* (to go), with a simple conjugation is *ibili* (to walk). The full set of the simple present tense is:

Ibili	***To walk***
Simple present tense	
Ni nabil	I walk
Hi habil	You (familiar) walk
Zu zabiltza	You (common singular) walk
Hura dabil	He, she, it walks
Gu gabiltza	We walk
Zuek zabiltzate	You (plural) walk
Haiek dabiltza	They walk

The direction suffix -raino

The suffix *-raino* (*-eraino* after consonants) is attached to common noun phrases in their indefinite form to yield the meaning 'until (reaching) that place', i.e. 'to that place' without actually entering it. It behaves exactly like *-ra* (lesson 9):

> *leihatila* counter > *leihatila**raino*** up to the counter
> *leku bat* a place > *leku bat**eraino*** until a place

The instrument suffix -z

The instrument by which a motion is performed is denoted by the suffix *-z* (*-ez* after consonants) often attached to the bare noun (the generalized instrument). We have already met a number of instances of this application: *abioiz* and *trenez* ('by plane' and 'by train' in lesson 3) and *oinez* and *autobusez* ('on foot' and 'by bus' in lesson 9). Similarly:

autoz and *kotxez* by car < *auto* or *kotxe* 'car'
untziz by ship < *untzi* 'ship'

The suffix is also used to indicate the medium through or across which the motion takes place:

airez through the air, by air < *aire* 'air'
bidez by road < *bide* 'road'

or a tool, an instrument of communication or observation, including the human senses:

aiztoz using a knife < *aizto* 'knife'
euskaraz in Basque (i.e. using Basque) < *euskara* 'Basque'
ingelesez in English < *ingeles* 'English'
lentez through a/the lens < *lente* 'lens'
begiz with the eye < *begi* 'eye'

The possessive adjectives

Most of the possessive adjectives have already made their appearance in the preceding dialogues. Here follows the complete set:

Possessive adjectives	
nire	my
hire	your (familiar)
zure	your (common singular possessor)
haren / bere	his, her, its
gure	our
zuen	your (plural possessor)
haien / beren	their

The difference between *haien* and *beren* is the same as between *haren* and *bere* (see lesson 7). Possessive adjectives are placed at the very beginning of the possessed noun phrase or occur as autonomous predicates where they must take the appropriate ending:

Gure hotel zaharra han dago; gurea da. There is our old hotel; it is ours.
Liburu hauek zuenak dira. These books are yours.

ADDITIONAL VOCABULARY

aire/a	air
auto/a	car, automobile
begi/a	eye
ber/a	(the) same, identical
denak	all
gelditu	to stop
hegazkin/a	airplane
ingeles/a	the English language
kotxe/a	car, automobile
lente/a	lens
untzi/a	ship

EXERCISES

Exercise 22: Translate into English.

1. Guk Baionan erreserbatu dugu hotel bat.
2. Oso lasai nago, geltokia hurbil baitago.
3. Atseginez ibiliko naiz zubiraino; bidea oso erosoa da.
4. Hotelak hogei gela ditu; denak handiak dira.
5. Hura gelan dabil: ez dago lasai.
6. Autoz ala trenez joango zara Bilbora? Autoz joango naiz.
7. Goizean ala arratsaldean iritsiko zara? Eguerdian iritsiko naiz.
8. Zer da hegazkina? Hegazkina edo abioia gauza bera da.
9. Hori, gauza oso txikia da; begiz ala lentez ikusi duzu?
10. Ni ez naiz ingelesez mintzatzen, euskaraz baizik.
11. Untzia itsasoz doa; hegazkina, ordea, airez.
12. Trena geltokian gelditzen da.
13. Trenak bidaia jarraituko du.
14. Bitartean guk gure ingelesezko elkarrizketa jarraitzen dugu.
15. Geltokiaren aurrean ilara luze bat dago, baina barruko ilara luzeagoa da.
16. Ilara kale ertzetik leihatilaraino doa.

Exercise 23: Translate into Basque.

1. Haven't you booked a hotel in Philadelphia?
2. He does not feel at ease because the theater is old.
3. We shall go up to the new theater by bus and from the theater we shall walk home.
4. There are ten cars in the street.
5. There are two telephones in the room.

6. I shall take the bus to go to San Sebastián; I am not in a hurry.
7. They take the ship to go from Bilbao to New York. They go by sea.
8. Which is your book? Is it the red one or the white one? They are all mine.
9. I spoke English on the telephone.
10. Is that book in Basque yours?
11. The bus takes the road until Guernica, but it does not stop in the small village.
12. The plane continues its flight to London.
13. I must buy my ticket, but the line is very long; it goes until the door.
14. Shall we speak Basque?
15. Tomorrow I shall continue the conversation; right now I am tired.
16. I shall walk up to school and shall stop at the florist's.

LESSON **ELEVEN**

HAMAIKAGGAREN IKASGAIA

ELKARRIZKETA

Zer ordutan helduko da trena?

Jone: Zer ordutan helduko da zure trena?
Pello: Ez dakit. Oraindik ez dut ordutegirik ikusi.
Jone: Begira! Egongelaren bazterrean pantaila handi bat dago. Ordutegia da.
Pello: Bai, ikusten dut. Goazen hara.
Jone: Zer erakusten du pantailak? Ez dut ongi ikusten. Letrak oso txikiak dira.
Pello: Nire trena hamarretan helduko da Bilbotik eta hamar eta erdietan aterako da Baionara. Ordu erdi batez geldituko da geltokian.
Jone: Pantailako trenak gaurkoak ala biharkoak dira?
Pello: Berdin da! Nire trena egunero pasatzen da. Eguneroko trena da eta beti ordu berean ateratzen da.
Jone: Kontuz! Ilararen burura iritsi gara. Orain leihatilaren aurrean gaude eta txartela erosi behar dugu.
Pello: Zer ordu da?! Bostak dira. Ordu batez itxaron behar ukan dugu!
Saltzailea: Nora joango zara?
Pello: Baionara. Txartel bat biharko, mesedez. Joatekoa bakarrik eta bigarren klasekoa.
Saltzailea: Tori! Hamabi euro, mesedez. Goizeko trena hamarretan pasatuko da.
Pello: Hori hartuko dut nik. Eskerrik asko!
Saltzailea: Bidaia on!

DIALOGUE

At what time will the train arrive?

Johanna: At what time will your train arrive?
Peter: I don't know. I have not seen any timetable yet.
Johanna: Look! In the corner of the waiting room there is a big screen. That is the timetable.
Peter: Yes, I see. Let us go there.
Johanna: What does the screen show? I do not see well. The letters are very small.
Peter: My train will arrive from Bilbao at ten and will leave for Bayonne at half past ten. It will stay at the station for thirty minutes.
Johanna: Are the trains on the screen for today or tomorrow?
Peter: It's the same! My train passes every day. It is a daily train and always leaves at the same time.
Johanna: Look out! (lit.: Attention!) We have come to the front (lit.: end) of the line. We now stand in front of the window and we must buy a ticket.
Peter: What time is it?! It is five o'clock. We have had to wait for an hour!
Ticket officer: Where will you be going?
Peter: To Bayonne. One ticket for tomorrow, please. One way only and second class.
Ticket officer: There you are! Twelve euros, please. The morning train will pass at ten.
Peter: That is the one I will take. Thanks a lot!
Ticket officer: Have a good trip!

VOCABULARY/HIZTEGIA

ordutegi/a	timetable
egongela	waiting room
bazter/ra	corner, edge
pantaila	screen
letra	letter (sign)
ordu (erdi) batez	for (half) an hour
atera	to leave
berdin	same
egunero	every day
pasatu	to pass
joateko/a	one-way ticket
klase/a	class

EXPRESSIONS/ESAERAK

Zer ordu da?	What time is it?
Zer ordutan?	At what time?
Badakizu …?	Do you know …?
Bai, badakit.	Yes, I know (it).
Ez, ez dakit.	No, I don't know (it).
Berdin da.	It's all the same.
Berdin zait.	It's the same to me, I don't care.
Berdin zaigu.	It's the same to us, we don't care.
Ordu berean.	At the same time (hour).
Aldi berean.	At the same time, simultaneously.
Kontuz!	Attention! Be careful! Watch out!

GRAMMAR

Telling the time

'What time is it?' is translated as *Zer ordu da?*, literally "What hour is it?" The question 'At what time?' is translated as *Zer ordutan?* The following table gives the answers to both questions in full hours:

In the same way 'half past' is translated by the cardinal number

What time is it?	***Zer ordu da?***	***At what time?***	***Zer ordutan?***
It is one o'clock.	**Ordu bata da.**	At one o'clock.	**Ordu batean.**
It is two o'clock.	**Ordu biak dira.**	At two o'clock.	**Ordu bietan.**
It is three o'clock.	**Hirurak dira.**	At three o'clock.	**Hiruretan.**
It is four o'clock.	**Laurak dira.**	At four o'clock.	**Lauretan.**
It is five o'clock.	**Bostak dira.**	At five o'clock.	**Bostetan.**
It is six o'clock.	**Seiak dira.**	At six o'clock.	**Seietan.**
It is seven o'clock.	**Zazpiak dira.**	At seven o'clock.	**Zazpietan.**
It is eight o'clock.	**Zortziak dira.**	At eight o'clock.	**Zortzietan.**
It is nine o'clock.	**Bederatziak dira.**	At nine o'clock.	**Bederatzietan.**
It is ten o'clock.	**Hamarrak dira.**	At ten o'clock.	**Hamarretan.**
It is eleven o'clock.	**Hamaikak dira.**	At eleven o'clock.	**Hamaiketan.**
It is twelve o'clock.	**Hamabiak dira.**	At twelve o'clock.	**Hamabietan.**
It is noon.	**Eguerdia da.**	At noon.	**Eguerdian.**
It is midnight.	**Gauerdia da.**	At midnight.	**Gauerdian.**

followed by *eta erdiak* (and a half), whereas 'at half past' is the cardinal number plus *eta erdietan* (and at a half). The following examples should be self-explanatory:

What time is it?	***Zer ordu da?***	***At what time?***	***Zer ordutan?***
Half past one.	**Ordu bat eta erdiak.**	At half past one.	**Ordu bat eta erdietan.**
Half past two.	**Ordu bi eta erdiak.**	At half past two.	**Ordu bi eta erdietan.**
Half past three.	**Hiru eta erdiak.**	At half past three.	**Hiru eta erdietan.**

and so on until twelve.

In exactly the same way the quarters past are formed by *eta laurdenak* (and a quarter) and *eta laurdenetan* (and at a quarter):

What time is it?	***Zer ordu da?***	***At what time?***	***Zer ordutan?***
A quarter past one.	**Ordu bat eta laurdenak.**	At a quarter past one.	**Ordu bat eta laurdenetan.**
A quarter past two.	**Ordu bi eta laurdenak.**	At a quarter past two.	**Ordu bi eta laurdenetan.**
A quarter past three.	**Hiru eta laurdenak.**	At a quarter past three.	**Hiru eta laurdenetan.**

and so on until twelve.

'A quarter to' is translated as the full hour expression followed by *laurden gutxi(ago)* (a quarter less), whereas 'at a quarter to' is the full hour followed by *laurden gutxi(ago)tan* (at a quarter less). The following examples should suffice (only the short forms are used):

What time is it?	***Zer ordu da?***	***At what time?***	***Zer ordutan?***
A quarter to one.	**Ordu bata laurden gutxi.**	At a quarter to one.	**Ordu bata laurden gutxitan.**
A quarter to two.	**Ordu biak laurden gutxi.**	At a quarter to two.	**Ordu biak laurden gutxitan.**
A quarter to three.	**Hirurak laurden gutxi.**	At a quarter to three.	**Hirurak laurden gutxitan.**

and so on until twelve.

The first thirty minutes after the full hour are indicated by the full hour followed by the numeral:

What time is it?	***Zer ordu da?***	***At what time?***	***Zer ordutan?***
Five past three.	**Hirurak eta bost.**	At five past three.	**Hirurak eta bostetan.**
Twenty past four.	**Laurak eta hogei.**	At twenty past four.	**Laurak eta hogeitan.**

The last thirty minutes before the full hour are expressed by *gutxi(ago)* (less):

What time is it?	***Zer ordu da?***	***At what time?***	***Zer ordutan?***
Five to three.	**Hirurak bost gutxi.**	At five to three.	**Hirurak bost gutxitan.**
Twenty to four.	**Laurak hogei gutxi.**	At twenty to four.	**Laurak hogei gutxitan.**

***The direction suffix* -rantz**

The suffix *-rantz* (*-erantz* after consonants) is attached to common noun phrases in their indefinite form to yield the meaning 'towards that place', i.e. 'in the global direction of that place'. It behaves exactly like *-ra* (lesson 9) and *-raino* (lesson 10):

> *leihatila* counter > *leihatila**rantz*** towards the counter
> *leku bat* a place > *leku bat**erantz*** towards a place

Complements of place

Basque has no prepositions like 'in', 'on', 'in front of', etc., to define the location of one object relative to the other. Instead, it makes use of the suffixes *-n* and *-an* (see lesson 3: *Gernikan* 'in Guernica' and lesson 9: *etxean* 'at home') attached to certain location nouns. These localizers follow the referred noun (phrase) instead of preceding it (like an English preposition does). The first five location nouns are repeated from lesson 9:

> *atze* backside > *atze**an*** at the backside, behind > *eliza**ren** atze**an*** behind the church
> *aurre* frontside > *aurre**an*** in front of > *etxe zuria**ren** aurre**an*** in front of the white house
> *barru* inside > *barru**an*** in, inside > *teatroa**ren** barru**an*** inside the theater
> *inguru* surroundings > *inguru**an*** in the surroundings > *gazteluaren**ren** inguru**an*** around the castle
> *kanpo* outer side > *kanpo**an*** outside > *hiri**tik** kanpo**(an)*** outside the city

In this last example, the form *kanpo* without *-an* is the more commonly used one in everyday speech. Note that all nouns or noun phrases to which the location is referred are placed in the genitive case (*-ren* after the definite form, see lesson 8) with the exception of nouns preceding *kanpoan*; these take the ending *-tik* after the indefinite form, indicating the separation between the two.

A few more cases are:

alde side > *alde***an** by the side of, next to > *eliza berria***ren** *alde***an** next to the new church

azpi underside > *azpi***an** under > *mahai zaharra***ren** *azpi***an** under the old table

bazter corner > *bazterre***an** in the corner > *egongela***ren** *bazterrean* in the corner of the waiting room

gain top > *gaine***an** on, on top of > *zaldia***ren** *gaine***an** on the horse

ondo side, vicinity > *ondo***an** by the side of, near > *neska***ren** *ondo***an** near the girl

pare face > *pare***an** facing > *etxea***ren** *pare***an** facing the house

Complements of time

The same location suffix *-an* (*-ean* after consonants) is used to locate an event in time, i.e. to form a complement of time. In the preceding lessons we have learned them in passing, e.g. in lesson 4: *arratsalde* > *arratsalde***an** (in the afternoon), *goiz* > *goize***an** (in the morning) and also *azken* > *azkene***an** (in the end). In this lesson we encountered *eguerdi***an** (at noon) and *ordu bere***an** (at the same hour).

ADDITIONAL VOCABULARY

alde/a	side
azpi/a	underside
gain/a	upper side, top
gaztelu/a	castle
irteera	exit, way out
ondo/a	side, vicinity
pare/a	facing side
sarrera	entrance
zaldi/a	horse
zergatik	why

EXERCISES

Exercise 24: Translate into English.

1. Orain zer ordu da?
2. Atzo zer ordutan etorri zen?
3. Bihar zer ordutan helduko da untzia?
4. Untzia eguerdian helduko da.
5. Goizeko zazpiak dira.
6. Arratsaldeko seiak dira.
7. Gaueko hamaikak dira.
8. Nire laguna zubirantz ibili zen.
9. Geltokiaren atzean eliza dago.
10. Gazteluaren inguruan etxeak ikusten ditut.
11. Zaldiaren gainean dago teatroaren barruan.
12. Autobusa geltokitik kanpo pasatzen da.
13. Pantaila sarreraren aurrean (or: parean) dago.
14. Ordutegia irteeraren ondoan zegoen.
15. Kontuz! Trena laster aterako da.
16. Berdin zait; ez nabil presaka eta ordu bete barru etorriko da beste tren bat.
17. Trena zergatik ez da geltokitik atera?
18. Ez dakit; ez dut trenik ikusi.

Exercise 25: Translate into Basque.

1. Is it two or three o'clock?
2. Did the plane yesterday arrive at midnight or at one in the morning?
3. This bus always passes at a quarter past eight.
4. A train leaves at the same hour.
5. We always have (take) breakfast at seven-thirty in the morning.
6. Do you have (take) lunch at two o'clock?
7. Dinner will be at nine in the evening.
8. The line goes from the entrance towards the box

office.

9. Behind our ship there is another one.
10. Outside the village I see the mountains.
11. There are flowers and plants in the corner of the store.
12. The big ship is at sea.
13. The station is facing my house.
14. The restaurant is near the river at the foot of the mountain.
15. Is it far from here?
16. We don't care: we are very hungry.
17. Why will he leave for San Sebastián tomorrow?
18. I know: his friend lives there.

LESSON **TWELVE**

HAMABIGARREN IKASGAIA

ELKARRIZKETA

Mendiko ibilaldi bat.

Jone:	Bihar Pellok Hegoaldea utziko du. Iparraldera joango da. Gu, ordea, hemen geldituko gara eta mendira igoko gara. Mendia oso atsegin zaigu.
Bernardo:	Ni ere etorriko naiz eta aita eta ama ere bai. Aitarekin eta amarekin txango polit bat egingo dugu. Diotenez eguraldia oso ederra izango da.
Jone:	Bai, bihar bero egingo du. Ez du haizerik edo euririk egingo, eguzkia baizik.
Bernardo:	Autoa hartuko dugu eta goizean goiz joango gara mendiaren oineraino. Han utziko dugu autoa eta oinez jarraituko dugu gora. Aparkalekutik gailurreraino igoko gara. Ibilaldia luzea izango da mendiko bideskaz.
Jone:	Gutxi gora-behera bi ordu barru gailurrera iritsiko gara. Handik ikuspegi zoragarria agertuko zaigu.
Bernardo:	Goizean beti lainoa egoten da mendian. Gero, eguzkitan, lainoa desagertuko da eta inguruan ikusiko ditugu zelai berdeak, txabolak eta ardiak. Alde batean harkaitz aldapatsuak agertuko zaizkigu eta beste aldean, urrunean, itsasoa.
Jone:	Gailurretik argazki batzuk egingo ditugu eta orduan beheratuko gara lehen herriko jatetxera. Bertan bazkalduko dugu. Amari oso atsegin zaio leku berde eta isil hura.
Bernardo:	Eta aitari atsegin zaio janaria.
Jone:	Horixe da! Denoi oso gustatuko zaigu biharko txangoa.

DIALOGUE

A walk in the mountains.

Johanna: Tomorrow Peter will leave the Southern Basque Country. He will go to the North. But we will stay here and go up to the mountains. We like the mountains very much.

Bernard: I will come too and Father and Mother as well. With Father and Mother we will have (lit.: make) a nice excursion. They say the weather will be very nice.

Johanna: Yes, tomorrow it will be hot. There won't be any wind or rain, but sunshine.

Bernard: We will take the car and go to the foot of the mountain early in the morning. There we will leave the car and continue the climbing on foot. We will go up from the parking lot to the mountain top. It will be a long walk along mountain trails.

Johanna: In about two hours we will get to the top. From there a fantastic view will appear in front of us.

Bernard: In the morning there is always mist in the mountains. Later, in the sunshine, the mist will disappear and we will see green pastures, cabins and sheep all around. On one side steep rocks will appear before us and on the other side, in the distance, the sea.

Johanna: We will take a few photographs from the top and then we will come down to the first restaurant in the village. There we will have lunch. Mother likes the green and quiet place a lot.

Bernard: And Father likes the food.

Johanna: Precisely! We will all enjoy tomorrow's outing.

VOCABULARY/HIZTEGIA

ibilaldi/a	walk
atsegin izan	to like, to be pleased
aita	father
ama	mother
txango/a	excursion, outing
egin	to do, to make
eguraldi/a	weather
bero egin	to be hot (the weather)
haize/a	wind
haizea egin	to be windy
euri/a	rain
euria egin	to rain
eguzki/a	sun
eguzkia egin	to be sunny
gora	higher up
aparkaleku/a	parking lot
gailur/ra	mountain top, peak
bideska	path, trail
gutxi gora-behera	about, approximately
handik	from there
ikuspegi/a	view, sight
zoragarri	fantastic
agertu	to appear
laino/a	mist, fog
eguzkitan	in the sunshine
desagertu	to disappear
zelai/a	pasture, field
berde	green
txabola	(shepherd's) cabin
ardi/a	sheep, ewe
harkaitz/a	rock
aldapatsu	steep
urrun/a	distant place
argazki/a	photograph, picture
argazkia egin	to take a picture
beheratu	to descend, come down
denoi	to all of us
gustatu	to like, to be pleased

EXPRESSIONS/ESAERAK

... oso atsegin zait.	I like ... very much.
... atsegin al zaizu?	Do you like ...?
Diotenez.	As they say, it is said.
Bero egiten du.	It is hot.
Hotz egiten du.	It is cold.
Gora eta behera.	Up and down.
... gustatzen zait.	I like ...
... gustatzen al zaizu?	Do you like ...?

GRAMMAR

The dative of izan *(to be)*

In lesson 11 we saw two instances of what we call the dative form of the verb 'to be': *Berdin zait* (It is the same to me) and *Berdin zaigu* (It is the same to us) and in this lesson's dialogue *Mendia oso atsegin zaigu* (We like the mountains a lot). In such cases the key person or subject in English (I or we) experiences a particular state or action, rather than causing it. The dative form of *izan* frequently occurs in expressions like 'it seems to me', 'I like it', 'it pleases me' and others where the key person exercises no control over the action, but simply undergoes it.

The following two tables list the complete sets for all persons with singular and plural subjects in Basque (objects in English). The dative forms of the pronouns (to me, to you, etc.) have the characteristic ending *-(r)i* but recall the same personal roots as the forms that we learned earlier (*ni* 'I', *nire* 'my', *niri* 'to me', etc.):

Izan	***To be***
Dative form, present tense, singular subject in Basque	
Niri (liburua) gustatzen zait	I like (the book)
Hiri (liburua) gustatzen zaik	You (familiar, male) like (the book)
Hiri (liburua) gustatzen zain	You (familiar, female) like (the book)
Zuri (liburua) gustatzen zaizu	You (common singular) like (the book)
Hari (liburua) gustatzen zaio	He, she likes (the book)
Guri (liburua) gustatzen zaigu	We like (the book)
Zuei (liburua) gustatzen zaizue	You (plural) like the book
Haiei (liburua) gustatzen zaie	They like (the book)

Izan	***To be***
Dative form, present tense, plural subject in Basque	
Niri (liburuak) gustatzen zaizkit	I like (the books)
Hiri (liburuak) gustatzen zaizkik	You (familiar, male) like (the books)
Hiri (liburuak) gustatzen zaizkin	You (familiar, female) like (the books)
Zuri (liburuak) gustatzen zaizkizu	You (common singular) like (the books)
Hari (liburuak) gustatzen zaizkio	He, she likes (the books)
Guri (liburuak) gustatzen zaizkigu	We like (the books)
Zuei (liburuak) gustatzen zaizkizue	You (plural) like (the books)
Haiei (liburuak) gustatzen zaizkie	They like (the books)

Bear in mind that the comparable literal translation would be "The book pleases me" and "The books please me." The infix *-zki-* denotes the plural subject in Basque (like *liburuak*), which often becomes an object in English.

Other examples are:

Ardo beltza atsegin zait. I like the red wine (it pleases me).
Loreak atsegin zaizkit. I like the flowers (they please me).

as well as other dative constructions:

Mendia agertzen zaigu. The mountain appears to us (in front of us).
Atea irekiko zaizu. The door will be opened to you.

The dative case -ri

The characteristic ending *-ri* of the dative case of the personal pronouns returns in the dative of common nouns, which is created by adding *-ri* to the definite. This suffix operates in exactly the same way as the genitive *-ren* (lesson 8):

> *gizona* the man > *gizona**ri*** to the man
> *neska* the girl > *neska**ri*** to the girl

The dative is the case which applies to the recipient of the action or the person who undergoes the action (the indirect object):

> *Txartela ematen zaio gizona**ri**.* The ticket is given to the man.
> *Loreak ematen zaizkio andrea**ri**.* The flowers are given to the lady.

The suffix -rekin *meaning '(together) with'*

The suffix *-rekin* attached to the definite form of a noun produces a complement introduced by '(together) with':

> *gizona* the man > *gizona**rekin*** with the man
> *neska* the girl > *neska**rekin*** with the girl

This suffix operates in exactly the same way as the dative *-ri* (above). This meaning of 'with' should not be confused with the 'with' that is sometimes used in the instrumental case:

> *nire autoaz* with my car (i.e. 'by my car' or 'in my car')

where it is the instrumental *-z* that is attached to the definite noun *autoa*.

Other prepositions

Notice the occurrence in the dialogue of *barru* (within) in the sentence *Bi ordu barru gailurrera iritsiko gara*, with *barru* not before but right after the noun *ordu* (hour). Compare also the dialogue in lesson 10: *ordu erdi barru* (within half an hour). From previous lessons we may also remember the preposition 'until' rendered by *arte* in:

Gero arte! See you later! (lit.: "later until")
Laster arte! See you soon! (lit.: "soon until")

Another example is *gabe* meaning 'without' or 'before, earlier than':

diru(rik) gabe without money
zu gabe without you
igandea gabe before Sunday
bihar gabe before tomorrow

Words like *barru*, *arte*, and *gabe* behave similar to the location nouns of lesson 11 (*aurrean*, *inguruan*, etc.). They all assume in Basque the role of prepositions as we know them in English.

Numerals/Zenbakiak (21–100, 1000)

Higher numbers in Basque are based on multiples of *twenty* rather than ten, repeating between multiples the sequence 1–20 that we learned already in lesson 7. The word *eta* (and) is fused with the preceding element: *hogei eta* … (twenty and …) > *hogeita* … The words *ehun* (one hundred) and *mila* (one thousand) are clearly outsiders in this system.

hogeita bat	twenty-one
hogeita bi	twenty-two
etc.	
hogeita hamar	thirty (twenty and ten)
hogeita hamaika	thirty-one (twenty and eleven)
etc.	
berrogei	forty (two twenties)
berrogeita hamar	fifty (two twenties and ten)
hirurogei	sixty (three twenties)
hirurogeita hamar	seventy (three twenties and ten)
laurogei	eighty (four twenties)
laurogeita hamar	ninety (four twenties and ten)
ehun	one hundred
mila	one thousand

Although very systematic, the system is difficult to process by someone used to the decimal system.

ADDITIONAL VOCABULARY

artalde/a	flock of sheep
artzain/a	shepherd
balio/a	value, worth
behera	down (direction)
eman	to give
Estatu Batuak	the United States
gabe	without, before (earlier than)
geratu	to stay, to be left
goxo/ak	candy
hodei/a	cloud
hotz egin	to be cold (weather)
ireki	to open
kilometro/a	kilometer
txakur/ra	dog

EXERCISES

Exercise 26: Translate into English.

1. Guk Estatu Batuak utzi ditugu eta Euskal Herrira heldu gara.
2. Estatu Batuak berrogeita hamabi dira.
3. Donostia Hegoaldean dago, baina Baiona Iparraldean.
4. Liburu hori oso gustatzen zait.
5. Koadro hura ez zaio gustatzen.
6. Gaurko eguraldia atsegin zaigu: bero egiten du.
7. Atzo haizea egin zuen; gaur goizean lainoa agertu zaigu itsasotik.
8. Mendiko bideskak gora eta behera doaz.
9. Artaldea zelaian dago; bertan dabil artzaina bere txakurrarekin.
10. Nire kotxea aparkalekuan dago.
11. Ez dago beste kotxerik: lekua hutsik eta isilik dago.
12. Ardo zuriak gustatzen zaizkit, baina beltzak ez zaizkit gustatzen.
13. Pastelak gustatuko zaizkio amari, baina goxoak ez zaizkio gustatuko.
14. Bernardo arrebarekin dator; elkarrekin teatrora doaz.
15. Hodei beltzak agertu zaizkigu; laster euria egingo du.
16. Denoi eguzkia atsegin zaigu.
17. Itsasora joango gara.
18. Zenbat kilometro geratzen dira herriraino? Herriraino hirurogeita zazpi kilometro geratuko dira.
19. Zenbat urte zituen zure aitak?
20. Aitak laurogei urte zituen.

Exercise 27: Translate into Basque.

1. Do you see that river over there? At the other end of the bridge is the Northern Basque Country.
2. We are leaving our home and going to the mountains.
3. We like the weather in the mountains, but we don't like the wind.
4. It is cold: it is not sunny today.
5. I like milk, but I don't like water. I always drink milk.
6. Does the new book please your father? No, he does not like it; he wants to buy the old one.
7. Thirty-five euros.
8. The value of the painting goes up and down.
9. The shepherd's cabin stands near the steep rock.
10. My mother's car leaves the parking lot.
11. There are lots of cars in the street, but few buses.
12. She likes the flowers and the plants, but they are expensive. They cost twenty-eight euros.
13. Will Johanna come with her brother?
14. Yes, together they will take the plane to go to Philadelphia.
15. I see small white clouds, but it will not rain until tomorrow.
16. They like the outing in the mountains and climb in the direction of the top.
17. They want to stop (break) on the steep trail.
18. Did you see that mountain in the distance? Its name is Txindoki.
19. Thirty kilometers are left up to the mountain.
20. By car we'll get there within half an hour.

APPENDIX **A**

APPENDIX A: How to Be Inventive in Basque

The Basque language has a number of so-called productive suffixes that can be used in combination with any candidate word from a particular class of words, as long as the result is meaningful. Thus, the combined knowledge of a limited number of lexical items (words) and that of a short list of suffixes gives the student a powerful way to actively create new words rather than learning them passively as new entities. In this appendix the beginning student of Basque is made familiar with this process through a small series of exercises in inventivity and pattern recognition. We'll explain the power of nine suffixes in the following sequence: six noun makers, two adjective makers and one verb maker.

Noun Makers

X-dun: *the person who is X*

X stands for any noun and the combination with *-dun* designates a person characterized by X:

> *ardura* responsibility > *ardura**dun*** responsible person
> *bizar* beard > *bizar**dun*** bearded man
> *fede* faith > *fede**dun*** believer

Exercise A1: Look up the applicable noun in the glossary and define the meaning of the following derived nouns:

> Example: *bizidun* living being < *bizi* life

1. errudun 2. hobendun 3. konkordun 4. zentzudun

Note also the slightly irregular form *zaldun* knight < *zaldi* horse.

X-keta: ***the 'X-ing'***

X stands for any verbal root and the derivative is a noun expressing an ongoing action whether this action produces a result or not:

> *aldatu* to change > *alda**keta*** alteration, modification
> *bilatu* to search > *bila**keta*** search
> *erabili* to use > *erabil**keta*** use, application
> *erosi* to buy > *eros**keta*** shopping

Exercise A2: Look up the applicable verb in the glossary and define the meaning of the following derived nouns:

> Example: *erakusketa* exhibition < *erakutsi* to show, display, exhibit

1. agurketa 2. ariketa 3. bihurketa 4. erorketa 5. garbiketa 6. ikasketa 7. konponketa 8. prestaketa 9. sendaketa 10. zuzenketa

X-le: ***the 'performer', 'habitual', or 'professional' of X***

X stands for the root of any transitive verb whose perfective ends with *-n* or *-i* preceded by *-r*, a vowel, a frictional consonant or an affricate. The result is a noun designating a (habitual) performer or professional often rendered in English by the suffix '-er', '-or', '-ant', and the like:

> *edan* to drink > *eda**le*** drinker
> *ekarri* to bring > *ekar**le*** bringer
> *erosi* to buy > *eros**le*** buyer
> *irakatsi* to teach > *irakas**le*** teacher

Note that the final *-n* of the verbal root is suppressed in these derivatives (*edale*) and that the affricate is reduced to its corresponding friction sound (*irakasle*).

Exercise A3: Look up the applicable verb in the glossary and define the meaning of the following derived nouns:

Example: *ebasle* thief < *ebatsi* to steal

1. egile 2. eragile 3. ereile 4. idazle 5. irakurle

X-tzaile: *the 'performer', 'habitual', or 'professional' of X*

In all those cases where *-le* does not apply (see above) the suffix *-tzaile* must be used:

aditu to listen > *adi**tzaile*** listener
sendatu to heal > *senda**tzaile*** healer
eho to mill > *eho**tzaile*** miller
hil to kill > *hil**tzaile*** killer
eraiki to build > *eraiki**tzaile*** builder

This suffix applies to the open class of verbs ending in *-tu* as well as to bare roots (like *eho)* and other perfectives ending in *-i* (like *eraiki*).

Exercise A4: Look up the applicable verb in the glossary and define the meaning of the following derived nouns:

Example: *askatzaile* liberator < *askatu* to liberate

1. azterzaile 2. erabiltzaile 3. jotzaile 4. jarraitzaile 5. pagatzaile

X-tasun: *abstract nouns*

X stands for any adjective, noun or pronoun and the derivative with *-tasun* designates an abstract noun with the property X, sometimes rendered in English by '-hood', '-ness', '-ship', '-th', or '-ty':

gazte young > *gazte**tasun*** youth
oso total > *oso**tasun*** totality
zabal wide > *zabal**tasun*** width, openness
nolako what kind of > *nolako**tasun*** quality

ama mother > *ama**tasun*** motherhood
adiskide friend > *adiskide**tasun*** friendship
gizon man > *gizon**tasun*** manliness

Exercise A5: Look up the applicable noun or adjective in the glossary and define the meaning of the following derived nouns:

Example: *maitetasun* love < *maite* beloved

1. edertasun 2. pobretasun 3. itsutasun 4. zuritasun 5. aitatasun 6. ugaritasun 7. haurtasun 8. etsaitasun 9. batasun 10. nortasun

X-tegi: *the place for X*

X stands for any noun and the combination with *-tegi* designates the location that is foreseen for or associated with X:

lan work > *lan**tegi*** workshop
liburu book > *liburu**tegi*** bookcase, library

Exercise A6: Look up the applicable noun or verb in the glossary and define the meaning of the following derived nouns:

Example: *apaiztegi* rectory < *apaiz* priest

1. ardotegi 2. auzitegi 3. eritegi 4. hobitegi 5. ikastegi

Note the more abstract derivations *egutegi* calendar < *egun* day, *hiztegi* dictionary < *hitz* word, and *ordutegi* timetable < *ordu* hour (lesson 11).

Adjective Makers

X-garri: *bringing about, sustaining or stimulating X*

X stands for any noun, adjective or verbal root, and the result of the combination is an adjective which can often be rendered by '-able' or 'worth -ing' or 'causing …' in English:

> *barre* laughter > *barre***garri** laughable ("making you laugh")
> *beldur* fear > *beldur***garri** frightening ("making you fear")
> *gogor* hard > *gogor***garri** hardening ("making hard")
> *urduri* nervous > *urduri***garri** worrying ("making nervous")
> *harritu* to wonder > *harri***garri** miraculous ("making you wonder")
> *indartu* to strengthen > *indar***garri** strengthening ("causing you to strengthen")
> *irakurri* to read > *irakur***garri** worth reading

Exercise A7: Look up the applicable noun, adjective or verb in the glossary and define the meaning of the following derived adjectives:

Example: *gupidagarri* pitiful ("causing pity") < *gupida* pity

1. damugarri 2. dudagarri 3. higuingarri 4. kaltegarri
5. berogarri 6. betegarri 7. erogarri 8. hordigarri
9. ezaugarri 10. galgarri 11. kutsagarri 12. trabagarri

X-tsu: *full of, rich in X*

X stands for any noun and the combination with *-tsu* produces an adjective with the meaning 'full of X', 'rich in X', 'with lots of X':

> *ahal* power > *ahal***tsu** powerful, mighty
> *balio* value > *balio***tsu** valuable
> *euri* rain > *euri***tsu** rainy
> *itzal* shadow > *itzal***tsu** shadowy
> *zarata* noise > *zarata***tsu** noisy

Exercise A8: Look up the applicable noun in the glossary and define the meaning of the following derived nouns:

Example: *aldapatsu* steep < *aldapa* slope

1. adintsu 2. arriskutsu 3. bizartsu 4. garrantzitsu 5. hodeitsu 6. ketsu 7. negartsu 8. odoltsu 9. oliotsu 10. sutsu

Verb Makers

X-tu: *verbs of all kinds*

The magic verb maker *-tu* attaches to all kinds of words and transforms these into verbs, both transitive and intransitive.

When *-tu* attaches to an adjective X the meaning is 'to make X' or 'to become X':

berri new > ***berritu*** to renew
gazte young > ***gaztetu*** to rejuvenate
lehor dry > ***lehortu*** to dry up

When *-tu* attaches to a noun X the meaning is 'to become X' or 'to end up X':

adiskide friend > ***adiskidetu*** to become friends
lurrin vapor > ***lurrindu*** to evaporate

Note the voice shift from *-tu* to *-du* in *lurrindu* caused by the final *-n* in *lurrin*.

When *-tu* attaches to a directional complement the meaning is 'to move to X':

aurrera forward > ***aurreratu*** to move forward, to promote
kanpora outside > ***kanporatu*** to go outside

Exercise A9: Look up the applicable noun or adjective in the glossary and define the meaning of the following derived verbs:

Example: *gaztetu* to rejuvenate < *gazte* young

1. gaixotu 2. isildu 3. mozkortu 4. zahartu 5. baketu 6. kezkatu 7. erregetu 8. poztu 9. atzeratu 10. bideratu 11. etxeratu 12. oheratu

APPENDIX B

APPENDIX B: Declension Summary

The following tables summarize the declension schemes of Basque nouns treated in the lessons 1 through 12. Each table gives in brackets the number of the lesson that discussed these declension schemes. A number of tables is added with declensions that were not discussed previously, but that are self-explanatory to the student who finished this very basic overview of the Basque grammar. They are distinguished by an asterisk in brackets.

Ergative case: transitive subject	
Singular	***Plural***
nik I (5)	**guk** we (5)
mutilak the boy (5)	**mutilek** the boys (5)

Genitive case: of, belonging to	
Singular reference	***Plural reference***
atearen of the door (8)	**ateen** of the doors (*)

Dative case: to	
Singular recipient	***Plural recipient***
gizonari to the man (12)	**gizonei** to the men (*)

Partitive case: indefiniteness in questions and negations	
ardorik wines, any wine (5)	**pastelik** cakes, any cake (5)

Of, in (expressing a general relation)

Singular geographical reference	*Plural geographical reference*
Bilboko Bilbao's (3)	**Ameriketako** American (3)

Singular common reference	*Plural common reference*
herriko of the country (3)	**herrietako** of the countries (*)
gaurko today's (3)	
hemengo from here, local (3)	

In, at, on (in a location)

Singular geographical reference	*Plural geographical reference*
Bilbon in Bilbao (3)	**Ameriketan** in America (3)

Singular common reference	*Plural common reference*
etxean in the house (9)	**etxeetan** in the houses (*)

To (general notion of direction)

Singular geographical reference	*Plural geographical reference*
Bilbora to Bilbao (3)	**Ameriketara** to America (3)

Singular common reference	*Plural common reference*
etxera to the house (9)	**etxeetara** to the houses (*)

From (general notion of separation)

Singular geographical reference	*Plural geographical reference*
Bilbotik from Bilbao (4)	**Ameriketatik** from America (4)

Singular common reference	*Plural common reference*
etxetik from the house (9)	**etxeetatik** from the houses (*)

Up to, until

Singular geographical reference	*Plural geographical reference*
Bilboraino up to Bilbao (*)	**Ameriketaraino** up to America (*)
Singular common reference	***Plural common reference***
etxeraino until the house (10)	**etxeetaraino** until the houses (*)

Towards, in the direction of

Singular geographical reference	*Plural geographical reference*
Bilborantz in the direction of Bilbao (*)	**Ameriketarantz** towards America (*)
Singular common reference	***Plural common reference***
etxerantz towards the house (11)	**etxeetarantz** towards the houses (*)

With, accompanied by

Singular reference	*Plural reference*
gizonarekin with the man (12)	**gizonekin** with the men (*)

By (general notion of instrument, tool, means)

Indefinite reference	*Singular reference*	*Plural reference*
abioiz by plane (10)	**nire abioiaz** by my plane (*)	**bere abioiez** by his planes (*)
autobusez by bus (10)		
airez by air (10)		
ingelesez in English (10)		

APPENDIX C

APPENDIX C: Conjugation Summary

The following tables summarize the conjugation schemes of Basque verbs treated in the lessons 1 through 12. These tabular overviews are limited to the essential references of each verb and to the first person singular and plural of its conjugation. Each table gives in brackets the number of the lesson that discussed these conjugation schemes.

The Intransitive Conjugation

The auxiliary and copula *izan* (to be)

Present tense (1)			
Ni naiz	I am	**Gu gara**	We are

Past tense (4)			
Ni nintzen	I was	**Gu ginen**	We were

Present tense, dative form			
Singular subject (12)		***Plural subject (12)***	
Niri zait	It is to me	**Niri zaizkit**	They are to me
Guri zaigu	It is to us	**Guri zaizkigu**	They are to us

The verb of state or whereabouts *egon* (to be)

Present tense (1)			
Ni nago	I am	**Gu gaude**	We are

Past tense (4)			
Ni nengoen	I was	**Gu geunden**	We were

The conjugation of intransitive verbs like *etorri* (to come)

(Habitual) present tense (6)	
Ni etortzen naiz	I come
Gu etortzen gara	We come

(Habitual) past tense (6)	
Ni etortzen nintzen	I came / used to come
Gu etortzen ginen	We came / used to come

Recent past tense (3)	
Ni etorri naiz	I came / have come
Gu etorri gara	We came / have come

Remote past tense (4)	
Ni etorri nintzen	I came / had come
Gu etorri ginen	We came / had come

Future tense (8)	
Ni etorriko naiz	I shall come
Gu etorriko gara	We shall come

The Transitive Conjugation

The auxiliary *ukan* (to have)

Present tense (5)			
Singular object		***Plural object***	
Nik dut	I have (it)	**Nik ditut**	I have (them)
Guk dugu	We have (it)	**Guk ditugu**	We have (them)

Past tense (5)			
Singular object		***Plural object***	
Nik nuen	I had (it)	**Nik nituen**	I had (them)
Guk genuen	We had (it)	**Guk genituen**	We had (them)

The conjugation of transitive verbs like *edan* (to drink)

(Habitual) Present tense (6)			
Singular object		***Plural object***	
Nik edaten dut	I drink (it)	**Nik edaten ditut**	I drink (them)
Guk edaten dugu	We drink (it)	**Guk edaten ditugu**	We drink (them)

(Habitual) Past tense (6)			
Singular object		***Plural object***	
Nik edaten nuen	I drank (it)	**Nik edaten nituen**	I drank (them)
Guk edaten genuen	We drank (it)	**Guk edaten genituen**	We drank (them)

Recent past tense (5)			
Singular object		***Plural object***	
Nik edan dut	I drank / have drunk (it)	**Nik edan ditut**	I drank / have drunk (them)
Guk edan dugu	We drank / have drunk (it)	**Guk edan ditugu**	We drank / have drunk (them)

Remote past tense (5)			
Singular object		***Plural object***	
Nik edan nuen	I drank / had drunk (it)	**Nik edan nituen**	I drank / had drunk (them)
Guk edan genuen	We drank / had drunk (it)	**Guk edan genituen**	We drank / had drunk (them)

Future tense (8)			
Singular object		***Plural object***	
Nik edango dut	I shall drink (it)	**Nik edango ditut**	I shall drink (them)
Guk edango dugu	We shall drink (it)	**Guk edango ditugu**	We shall drink (them)

Simple conjugations (intransitive)

Etorri	***To come***
Present tense (9)	
Ni nator	I come / am coming
Gu gatoz	We come / are coming

Joan	***To go***
Present tense (9)	
Ni noa	I go / am going
Gu goaz	We go / are going

Ibili	***To walk***
Present tense (10)	
Ni nabil	I walk / am walking
Gu gabiltza	We walk / are walking

Simple conjugations (transitive)

Eduki		***To hold***	
Present tense (7)			
Singular object		***Plural object***	
Nik daukat	I hold (it)	**Nik dauzkat**	I hold (them)
Guk daukagu	We hold (it)	**Guk dauzkagu**	We hold (them)

EXERCISEKEY

EXERCISE KEY

Note: sometimes more than one solution is possible, but only one is given; consult the grammar in case of doubt.

Exercise 1:
/s'ágar/, /s'águ/, /emákume/, /éder/, /góna/, /górri/, /(h)ándi/, /tshíki/, /mútil/, /jáwna/, /ewría/, /ews'kára/, /áyta/, /(h)ógey/, /goy/, /be(h)y/, /trés'na/, /argía/, /akérra/, /nagús'ia/, /sáldi/, /belts/, /s'orgínya/, /apáysa/, /ashóla/, /(h)ots/, /átso/, /améts'a/, /tshar/, /tshoría/, /bí(h)ots/.

Exercise 2:
senar, soka, euskalduna, uda, gerra, handitasuna, txirla, bonbil, jauntxo, elurra, aitona, hirurogei, gai, ehiza, asko, haserre, eltze, eltxo, zoriona, haizea, kutxa, utzi, jatetxe, zaharra, txaloa, ahazti.

Exercise 3:
1. Good morning! I am a boy. 2. Good afternoon! Are you Bernard? 3. Hi! I am a girl. 4. Who are you? 5. I am Johanna. 6. It is a nice name. 7. I am very glad. See you later! 8. Who is she? She is Anna. Anna is a woman. 9. Johanna is a young lady. 10. And who are you? I am Michael. I am a man. 11. You are glad. 12. The gentleman is very happy.

Exercise 4:
1. Kaixo! Zure izena Miren da? 2. Arratsalde on, ni Miren naiz. 3. Jone mutila da? 4. Jone neska da. 5. Egun polita da. 6. Eguna polita da. 7. Mikel nire neba da. 8. Ane zure arreba da. 9. Nor da hura? Bernardo da. Gizona da. 10. Eta hura nor da? Jone da. Andereñoa da. 11. Hura oso pozik dago. 12. Anderea ere pozik dago.

Exercise 5:

1. Where is Bernard? 2. Bernard is over there. 3. How is he? 4. He is well. 5. Maria is sick. 6. Johanna is tired. 7. Here is a boy. 8. The book is white. 9. The other book is red. 10. The notebook is also red. 11. Here are some girls. 12. The names are not pretty. 13. The girl is tired. 14. Bernard is not Johanna's companion: he is Johanna's brother. 15. Maria, on the contrary, is Johanna's companion. 16. Johanna and Maria are friends.

Exercise 6:

1. Non daude Bernardo eta Miren? 2. Han daude. 3. Nola zaudete? 4. Ondo gaude. 5. Hona hemen beste mutil bat. 6. Mikel nire adiskidea da. 7. Ane oso nekaturik dago. 8. Nire laguna gaixorik dago. 9. Neskak oso politak dira. 10. Hona hemen liburu eta koaderno batzuk. 11. Beste liburua ez dago hemen. 12. Begira, zuria hemen dago! 13. Jone Bernardoren arreba da. 14. Miren, ordea, ez da Bernardoren arreba. 15. Miren Joneren laguna da. 16. Haiek lagunak dira.

Exercise 7:

1. Bai, ni Jone naiz. 2. Ez, ni ez naiz mutila. 3. Bai, nire izena Bernardo da. 4. Bai, izen polita da. 5. Bai, neska polita da. 6. Ez, ez dago han. 7. Bai, han daude. 8. Ez, hura ez dago nekaturik. 9. Bai, mutil ona da. 10. Ez, ni ez nago gaixorik. 11. Bai, liburua zuria da. 12. Ez, liburuak ez daude han. 13. Ez, koadernoa ez da gorria. 14. Bai, Ane nire laguna da. 15. Ez, gu ez gara lagunak. 16. Bai, Mikel nire neba da.

Exercise 8:

1. Where is the boy from? He is from Bilbao. 2. When did he come to America? He came today. 3. Where do the girls

live? The girls live in Guernica. 4. Do you live in Guernica too? 5. No, I don't live in Guernica. I live in Bayonne. 6. Guernica is in "the South." 7. Bayonne is in "the North." 8. When did the train go to London? The train went today. 9. Is this your first visit? No, this is not my first visit. 10. This is my second trip. 11. When did the plane arrive? The plane did not arrive. 12. Do you live in the Basque Country or in America? 13. We live in America; we are Americans. 14. Where is Bilbao? 15. Bilbao is in the Southern Basque Country. 16. Where are the women from? The women are from "the North."

Exercise 9:
1. Nongoak dira neskak? Baionakoak dira. 2. Noiz etorri zarete Gernikara? Gaur heldu gara. 3. Non bizi da gizona? Gizona Iparraldean bizi da. 4. Zu ere Iparraldean bizi zara? 5. Ez, ni Hegoaldean bizi naiz; Bilbon bizi naiz. 6. Gernika Hegoaldeko herria da. 7. Baiona Iparraldeko hiria da. 8. Abioia noiz joan da New Yorkera? Abioia gaur joan da. 9. Hau zure lehen ala bigarren bidaia da? 10. Hau nire lehen bisita da. 11. Trena Bilbora heldu da? Ez, ez da heldu. 12. Haiek Kaliforniara etorri dira? 13. Bai, Kaliforniakoak dira. 14. Non zaude? 15. Hemen nago; hona etorri naiz. 16. Nongoak dira mutilak? Hangoak dira.

Exercise 10:
1. Where is your house? My house is over there. 2. Our trip was very pleasant. 3. Where did the train arrive from? The train arrived from San Sebastián. It arrived yesterday morning. 4. Where did the train go to? The train went to Biarritz. It went yesterday afternoon. 5. Where is the station in Bilbao? The station is in the city center. 6. Where are the churches in San Sebastián? The churches in San Sebastián are over there. 7. The restaurant is very big. 8. The cities in the Basque Country are very interesting. 9. What happened

yesterday in Guernica? 10. I was not in Guernica yesterday. 11. Where were you born? 12. I was born in America. 13. Is the book pleasant or boring? The book is pleasant. 14. We walked to this place; we were tired. 15. From where to where did you walk? 16. We walked from San Sebastián to Guernica.

Exercise 11:

1. Non dago jatetxea? Jatetxea hor dago! 2. Nire bigarren bisita oso atsegina zen. 3. Nondik etorri zen abioia? Abioia Parisetik heldu zen. Atzo heldu zen. 4. Nora joan zen abioia? Londresera joan zen abioia. 5. Non zaudete? Gu erdialdean gaude. 6. Geltokia hor dago? Bai, hemen dago. 7. Eliza eta jatetxea han daude. 8. Hemengo bidea oso luzea da; nekaturik gaude. 9. Hiria ikusgarria al da? Bai, herri interesgarria da. 10. Atzo zer gertatu zen Donostian? 11. Atzo gu Miarritzen geunden. 12. Hura Iparraldean jaio zen? Ez, Hegoaldean jaio zen. 13. Ni Iparraldetik Hegoaldera joan nintzen; bidaia interesgarria izan zen. 14. Zu Bizkaian zeunden? 15. Ez, ez nengoen Bizkaian; denbora gutxian egon nintzen Hegoaldean. 16. Atzoko hegaldi luzea aspergarria izan zen.

Exercise 12:

1. I am hungry. I want to eat a piece of cake. 2. Maria was thirsty. Maria wanted to drink water. 3. Have you had any coffee? 4. No, we have not had any coffee. 5. Did you see the small cup? 6. Yes, I saw the cup. 7. No, I did not see the cup; I did not see any cup. 8. What is that thing? This is a cup of coffee. 9. And what is that other thing? 10. I have not seen anything. 11. I want to eat a few cakes and I want to drink milk. 12. They had taken the cakes. 13. We want to take one book. 14. He had drunk much wine. 15. I had taken some glasses or bowls. 16. You have seen the boys. 17. Have you drunk the water? 18. Yes, I have drunk

the water; I have drunk cold water. 19. No, I have not drunk any water. 20. I was not thirsty; the glass stands empty. 21. Is there any milk? 22. Are there books?

Exercise 13:
1. Gu egarri gara. Guk ura edan nahi dugu. 2. Bernardo gose zen. Bernardok pastel batzuk jan nahi zituen. 3. Haiek terik hartu al dute? 4. Bai, haiek tea hartu dute. 5. Adiskiderik ikusi al zuen? 6. Ez, ez zuen adiskiderik edo lagunik ikusi. 7. Mutilak eta neskak joan ziren. 8. Zer da hori? Hori ura ala ardo zuria al da? 9. Ez dut ezer ikusi. 10. Hark esnea nahi zuen edateko. 11. Zuek gose zarete; ogirik nahi duzue jateko? 12. Ogia hartu genuen. 13. Hark koa-derno bat hartu nahi du. 14. Atzo ardo asko edan genuen. 15. Edontziak, kikarak eta katiluak ikusi ditut. 16. Liburua hartu nahi nuen. 17. Neskak ikusi al dituzue? 18. Bai, ikusi ditut. 19. Ez, ez dut neskarik ikusi. 20. Atzo ez nintzen gose; ez nuen ezer jan. 21. Badago urik? 22. Ba al dago kikararik?

Exercise 14:
1. Do you take any meat? 2. No, we do not take any meat. 3. Do you see the bottle? 4. Yes, I see the bottle. 5. No, I do not see the bottle; I do not see any bottle. 6. What is that thing? This is a bottle of wine. It is red wine. 7. And what is that other thing? 8. I do not see anything. 9. They bring the dishes. 10. We take the forks and the knives. 11. He drinks a lot of wine; before he used to drink little wine. 12. I eat many vegetables. 13. There is beer and cider in the kitchen; there is no wine over there. 14. What kind of wine is that? 15. This one is red; the one over there is not red; it is white. 16. There is beer on the table. 17. Is that beer good? 18. It is very good indeed. 19. What is happening over there? 20. Nothing is happening over there. 21. They always went by train to Bayonne. 22. You used to come here many times.

Exercise 15:

1. Hark esnerik hartzen du? 2. Ez, ez du esnerik hartzen; zizka-mizkak hartzen ditu. 3. Haiek platerak ikusten dituzte mahaian? 4. Bai, platerak ikusten dituzte. 5. Nik, ordea, ez ditut platerak ikusten; ez dut ezer ikusten. 6. Zer eka-rri du? Sardeskak, koilarak eta aiztoak ekarri ditu. 7. Eta zer da hori? 8. Hau sagardoa da; gaur goizean erosi dugu. 9. Ardoa atzo erosi genuen. 10. Haiek haragi asko jaten zuten. 11. Gaur ez dute haragirik jaten. 12. Zuk beti barazkiak jaten dituzu? 13. Guk askotan edaten dugu garagardoa edo esnea. 14. Kaixo! Hori ardo zuria al da? 15. Arratsalde on! Ez, hau ura da. 16. Ardoa sukaldean dago oraindik. 17. Zer da hura? 18. Haiek zizka-mizkak dira; Mirenek prestatu ditu gaur goizean. 19. Zer erosten zuen? 20. Liburu asko erosten zituen. 21. Askotan etortzen ginen hona. 22. Haiek beti trenez joaten dira Donostira.

Exercise 16:

1. How much money does he need? He needs twenty euros. 2. He needs much money; he is not a rich man. 3. The flowers are not expensive; we have bought beautiful roses. 4. Have you seen Maria? 5. She is selling flowers. There is her store. 6. That plant is not cheap. 7. We have not bought any plants: those flowers are cheaper. 8. How many euros do you have in your pocket? 9. I have ten euros: I have a ten euro note in my pocket. 10. What do they sell? They sell flowers. 11. Is this money enough to buy the flowers? 12. Yes, that money is enough. 13. There you are, two banknotes and a few coins! 14. We want to buy those roses: they are beautiful and very fresh. They are not ugly. 15. The salesperson used to sell fresh flowers; here roses were very nice. 16. I must look for the money in my pocket; I have not found any banknotes or coins. 17. Do you have money in your pocket? 18. Do you have dishes in the kitchen?

Exercise 17:

1. Zuk dirurik al daukazu sakelan? Ez daukat dirurik. 2. Diru gutxi behar dut: ez naiz gizon behartsua. 3. Hemengo loreak eta landareak merkeak dira; hamazazpi arrosa erosi nahi ditugu. 4. Jone ikusten al duzu han? Bera saltzailea da! 5. Haiek liburuak eta koadernoak saltzen zituzten. 6. Ardo hori ez da merkea, oso garestia baizik: hamabi euro balio du. 7. Guk ez genuen ezer erosten. 8. Zuk bost euroko bileterik al daukazu sakelan? 9. Bai, tori! Baina nik bost euroko bilete bat bakarrik daukat. 10. Benetan liburuak saltzen ditu? 11. Hamar euroko bilete bat nahikoa da botila ardo hau erosteko. 12. Ez da nahikoa liburu eder hura erosteko. 13. Begira! Hona hemen hogei euroko bilete bat eta txanpon batzuk ere bai. 14. Koaderno txiki hauek erosi nahi ditut. 15. Etxe handiak erosten zituen. 16. Nik, ordea, etxe txiki polit bat bilatzen dut. 17. Baduzu lorerik? 18. Baduzu txanponik sakelan?

Exercise 18:

1. How many days does a week have? A week has seven days. 2. How many weeks does a month have? Four weeks. 3. A year has four seasons. 4. Yesterday you came home very late, as always. 5. We always come home late. 6. This morning we came home in time. 7. Tomorrow we shall also come in time. 8. Thursday is the fourth day of the week. As always we are working. 9. Tomorrow we shall be working too. It will be Friday, the fifth day. 10. The day after tomorrow we shall not be working. It will be the weekend and we shall be free. 11. A working day is not a special day. 12. Sunday is a special day: we are (always) free. 13. Today is the first day of the month, but tomorrow will be the last day of the year. 14. The day after tomorrow, however, will be the first day of the year. 15. The first of the year is (always) a holiday. 16. I have not yet read this book; tomorrow I shall read it.

Exercise 19:

1. Asteak bost egun ditu? Ez, asteak bost lanegun ditu. 2. Hilaren asteak lau dira. 3. Hau urtearen lehen urtaroa da. 4. Iaz lore ederrak erosi genituen. 5. Askotan erosten genituen loreak. 6. Gaur arratsaldean loreak eta landareak erosi ditugu. 7. Bihar ez dugu ezer erosiko. 8. Astelehena astearen lehen eguna da. 9. Bihar asteartea izango da; laneguna izango da, gaur bezala. 10. Atzo igandea izan zen, egun berezia. 11. Igandea asteburuaren bigarren eguna da; lehena larunbata da. 12. Mutila eskolara joaten da: gaur ez da jaieguna. 13. Etxeak hiru ate ditu, eta ate batek bakarrik giltza du. 14. Atearen giltza bilatzen dut. 15. Giltza non zegoen? 16. Giltza sukaldean zegoen.

Exercise 20:

1. Yesterday I saw (visited) your village. 2. That place is in the countryside. 3. We go from the hotel to the theater. 4. We all were in the theater. 5. The inside of the theater is very nice, but the outside is ugly. 6. There are mountains around the city. 7. Tomorrow we shall go (up) from the city to the mountains. 8. The river goes from the mountains to the sea. 9. You are on the bridge and you see the city center. 10. Right now we go the city square and we shall see the arches. 11. To the right you have the front of the church. 12. To the left there was the rearside of the old station. 13. We always go on foot from home to the jai alai court: we walk. 14. In the distance I see the mountains. 15. The day after tomorrow I shall go there. 16. The sea is not so nearby.

Exercise 21:

1. Etzi denok Baiona ikusiko dugu. 2. Hiria ibaiaren ertzean dago. 3. Haiek etxetik geltokira datoz. 4. Hura pilotalekuan zegoen. 5. Herriaren ingurua ederra da. 6. Urruti itsasoa ikusten duzu. 7. Gaur mendira goaz. 8.

Denok elkarrekin bazkalduko duzue. 9. Ni enparantzan nengoen eta oroitarria ikusi nuen. 10. Etorbidea oso zabala da. 11. Nire etxea ezkerrera dago; eliza eskuinera dago. 12. Elizatik zubira ibiliko gara. 13. Itsasora autobusez joaten gara beti. 14. Zure hotela hurbil dago. 15. Iaz hotelean afaldu zuten. 16. Mendialdeko etxe zaharrean bizi gara.

Exercise 22:

1. We have booked a hotel in Bayonne. 2. I feel very comfortable because the station is nearby. 3. I shall walk up to the bridge with pleasure; the road is very easy. 4. The hotel has twenty rooms; they are all big. 5. He walks in the room: he is not at ease. 6. Will you go to Bilbao by car or by train? I shall go by car. 7. Will you arrive in the morning or late in the afternoon? I shall arrive at noon. 8. What is a hegazkina (airplane)? Hegazkina (airplane) or abioia (airplane) is the same thing. 9. That is a very small thing; have you seen it with the eye or by a lens? 10. I do not speak English, but Basque. 11. The ship goes by sea; the plane, on the contrary, goes through the air. 12. The train stops at the station. 13. The train will continue its journey. 14. Meanwhile we continue our conversation in English. 15. There is a long line in front of the station, but the line inside is longer. 16. The line goes from the curb up to the counter.

Exercise 23:

1. Ez al duzu hotelik erreserbatu Filadelfian? 2. Hura ez dago lasai, antzokia zaharra baitago. 3. Autobusez joango gara teatro berriraino eta teatrotik ibiliko gara etxera. 4. Kalean hamar kotxe daude. 5. Gelan bi telefono daude. 6. Autobusa hartuko dut Donostiara joateko; ez nabil presaka. 7. Haiek untzia hartzen dute Bilbotik New Yorkera joateko. Itsasoz doaz. 8. Zein da zure liburua? Gorria da,

ala zuria? Denak nireak dira. 9. Telefonoz ingelesez mintzatzen nintzen. 10. Euskarazko liburu hori zurea al da? 11. Autobusak bidea hartzen du Gernikaraino, baina ez da herri txikian gelditzen. 12. Hegazkinak jarraitzen du hegaldia Londresera. 13. Nire txartela erosi behar dut, baina ilara oso luzea da; ateraino doa. 14. Euskaraz mintzatuko gara? 15. Bihar jarraituko dut elkarrizketa; oraintxe nekaturik nago. 16. Eskolaraino ibiliko naiz eta loradendan geldituko naiz.

Exercise 24:
1. What time is it now? 2. At what time did she come yesterday? 3. At what time will the ship arrive tomorrow? 4. The ship will arrive at noon. 5. It is seven o'clock in the morning. 6. It is six in the afternoon. 7. It is eleven in the evening. 8. My friend walked towards the bridge. 9. Behind the station is the church. 10. I see the houses around the castle. 11. He sits on a horse inside the theater. 12. The bus passes outside the station. 13. The screen is in front of the entrance. 14. The timetable was (located) near the exit. 15. Careful! The train will leave shortly. 16. I don't care; I am not in a hurry and within one hour there will be another train. 17. Why has the train not left the station? 18. I don't know; I haven't seen any train.

Exercise 25:
1. Ordu biak ala hirurak dira? 2. Atzoko hegazkina gauerdian ala goizeko ordu batean heldu zen? 3. Autobus hau zortziak eta laurdenetan pasatzen da beti. 4. Ordu berean tren bat joaten da. 5. Guk beti zazpi eta erdietan hartzen dugu gosaria. 6. Zuk ordu bietan bazkaltzen duzu? 7. Afaria gaueko bederatzietan izango da. 8. Ilara sarreratik leihatilarantz doa. 9. Gure untziaren atzean beste bat dago. 10. Herritik kanpo mendiak ikusten ditut. 11. Loradendaren bazterrean loreak eta landareak daude. 12.

Untzi handia itsasoan dago. 13. Geltokia nire etxearen parean dago. 14. Jatetxea ibai ondoan dago, mendiaren oinean. 15. Hemendik urruti al dago? 16. Berdin zaigu: oso gose gara. 17. Zergatik aterako da bihar Donostiara? 18. Badakit: bere laguna bertan bizi da.

Exercise 26:

1. We have left the United States and have arrived in the Basque Country. 2. There are fifty-two states in the United States. 3. San Sebastián is in the Southern Basque Country, but Bayonne is in the North. 4. I like that book a lot. 5. He does not like that painting. 6. We like the weather today: it is hot. 7. Yesterday it was windy; this morning a fog has come up from the sea. 8. The mountain trails go up and down. 9. The flock of sheep is in the pasture; the shepherd is walking there with his dog. 10. Our car is in the car park. 11. There are no other cars: the place is empty and silent. 12. I like white wines, but I don't like red ones. 13. Mother will like the cakes, but she will not like the candy. 14. Bernard is coming with his sister; they go together to the theater. 15. Black clouds have appeared in front of us; it will soon rain. 16. We all like the sun. 17. We shall go to the sea. 18. How many kilometers are left to the village? There will be sixty-seven kilometers left up to the village. 19. How old was your father? 20. My father was eighty years old.

Exercise 27:

1. Ibai hura ikusten duzu? Zubiaren beste aldean Iparraldea dago. 2. Etxea uzten dugu eta mendira goaz. 3. Mendiko eguraldia atsegin zaigu, baina ez zaigu atsegin haizea. 4. Hotz egiten du: gaur ez du eguzkirik egiten. 5. Esnea gustatzen zait, baina ez zait gustatzen ura. Beti esnea edaten dut. 6. Liburu berria zure aitari gustatzen zaio? Ez, ez zaio gustatzen; zaharra erosi nahi du. 7. Hogeita hamabost euro. 8.

Koadroaren balioa gora eta behera doa. 9. Txabola harkaitz aldapatsuaren ondoan dago. 10. Amaren kotxeak aparkalekua uzten du. 11. Kalean kotxe asko daude, baina autobus gutxi. 12. Loreak eta landareak gustatzen zaizkio, baina garestiak dira. Hogeita zortzi euro balio dute. 13. Jone bere nebarekin etorriko al da? 14. Bai, elkarrekin hegazkina hartuko dute Filadelfiara joateko. 15. Hodei txiki zuriak ikusten ditut, baina bihar arte ez du euririk egingo. 16. Mendiko txangoa atsegin zaie eta gailurrerantz igotzen dira. 17. Bideska aldapatsuan gelditu nahi dute. 18. Urruti (Urrunean) ikusi al duzu mendi hura? Bere izena Txindoki da. 19. Hogeita hamar kilometro geratzen dira mendiraino. 20. Autoz ordu erdi bat barru iritsiko gara hara.

Exercise A1:

1. *errudun* guilty (one) < *erru* guilt 2. *hobendun* sinner < *hoben* sin 3. *konkordun* hunchback < *konkor* hunch 4. *zentzudun* sensible person < *zentzu* sense

Exercise A2:

1. *agurketa* the greeting < *agurtu* to greet 2. *ariketa* exercise, activity < *aritu* to be busy doing 3. *bihurketa* restitution < *bihurtu* to return 4. *erorketa* fall < *erori* to fall 5. *garbiketa* the cleaning < *garbitu* to clean 6. *ikasketa* study < *ikasi* to study 7. *konponketa* repair, fixing < *konpondu* to repair, to fix 8. *prestaketa* preparation < *prestatu* to prepare 9. *sendaketa* the healing < *sendatu* to heal, to cure 10. *zuzenketa* correction < *zuzendu* to correct

Exercise A3:

1. *egile* maker, author < *egin* to make 2. *eragile* promoter < *eragin* to promote, to boost 3. *ereile* sower < *erein* to sow 4. *idazle* writer < *idatzi* to write 5. *irakurle* reader < *irakurri* to read

Exercise A4:

1. *azterzaile* examiner < *aztertu* to examine 2. *erabiltzaile* user < *erabili* to use 3. *jotzaile* musician, player < *jo* to play music 4. *jarraitzaile* follower < *jarraitu* to follow 5. *pagatzaile* payer < *pagatu* to pay

Exercise A5:

1. *edertasun* beauty < *eder* beautiful 2. *pobretasun* poverty < *pobre* poor 3. *itsutasun* blindness < *itsu* blind 4. *zuritasun* whiteness < *zuri* white 5. *aitatasun* fatherhood < *aita* father 6. *ugaritasun* abundance < *ugari* abundant 7. *haurtasun* childhood < *haur* child 8. *etsaitasun* enmity < *etsai*

enemy 9. *batasun* unity < *bat* one 10. *nortasun* personality < *nor* who

Exercise A6:

1. *ardotegi* wine cellar < *ardo* wine 2. *auzitegi* courthouse < *auzi* lawsuit 3. *eritegi* infirmary < *eri* sick person 4. *hobitegi* cemetery < *hobi* tomb 5. *ikastegi* school < *ikasi* to learn, to study

Exercise A7:

1. *damugarri* regrettable < *damu* regret 2. *dudagarri* doubtful < *duda* doubt 3. *higuingarri* repugnant, disgusting < *higuin* disgust 4. *kaltegarri* harmful, damaging < *kalte* damage 5. *berogarri* heat keeping < *bero* heat 6. *betegarri* filling < *bete* full 7. *erogarri* maddening < *ero* mad 8. *hordigarri* intoxicant < *hordi* drunk, intoxicated 9. *ezaugarri* characteristic, distinctive < *ezagutu* to know, to distinguish 10. *galgarri* ruinous < *galdu* to lose, to ruin 11. *kutsagarri* contaminating, contagious < *kutsatu* to contaminate, to infect 12. *trabagarri* troubling < *trabatu* to hinder, to obstruct

Exercise A8:

1. *adintsu* elderly < *adin* age 2. *arriskutsu* risky, dangerous < *arrisku* risk, danger 3. *bizartsu* bearded < *bizar* beard 4. *garrantzitsu* important < *garrantzi* importance 5. *hodeitsu* clouded < *hodei* cloud 6. *ketsu* smoky < *ke* smoke 7. *negartsu* tearful < *negar* tear 8. *odoltsu* bloody < *odol* blood 9. *oliotsu* oily < *olio* oil 10. *sutsu* fiery, burning < *su* fire

Exercise A9:

1. *gaixotu* to make/get sick < *gaixo* sick 2. *isildu* to shut up < *isil* silent 3. *mozkortu* to get drunk < *mozkor* drunk 4. *zahartu* to get old(er) < *zahar* old 5. *baketu* to pacify < *bake* peace 6. *kezkatu* to worry < *kezka* worry, concern 7. *erregetu* to make king < *errege* king 8. *poztu* to enjoy < *poz* joy 9. *atzeratu* to retreat < *atzera* backwards 10. *bideratu* to take to the road < *bidera* to the road 11. *etxeratu* to go home < *etxera* home 12. *oheratu* to go/put to bed < *ohera* to bed

GLOSSARY BASQUE-ENGLISH

GLOSSARY BASQUE-ENGLISH

The numbers in brackets after an entry in Basque refer to the lesson in which the word appeared for the first time; (A) refers to the appendix A.

aberats (7)	rich
abioi/a (3)	airplane
abioiz (3)	by plane
adin/a (A)	age
adiskide/a (2)	friend
adiskidetasun/a (A)	friendship
adiskidetu (A)	to become friends
aditu (A)	to listen
aditzaile/a (A)	listener
afaldu (9)	to dine
afari/a (6)	dinner, late evening meal
agertu (12)	to appear
agur (1)	bye, good-bye
agurtu (A)	to greet
ahal/a (A)	power
ahaltsu (A)	powerful
aire/a (10)	air
aita (12)	father
aizto/a (6)	knife
al (4)	interrogative particle (untranslated)
ala (3)	or
aldaketa (A)	alteration, modification
aldapa (A)	slope
aldapatsu (12)	steep
aldatu (A)	to change
alde/a (11)	side
aldi/a (11)	time, span, period
ama (12)	mother
amatasun/a (A)	motherhood
Amerika (3)	America

amerikar/ra (3)	American
andere/a (1)	lady, Mrs.
andereño/a (1)	young lady, Miss
antzoki/a (9)	theater
apaiz/a (A)	priest
apaiztegi/a (A)	rectory
aparkaleku/a (12)	parking lot
ardi/a (12)	sheep, ewe
ardo/a (5)	wine
ardura (A)	responsibility
arduradun/a (A)	responsible person
argazki/a (12)	photograph, picture
argazkia egin (12)	to take a picture
aritu (A)	to be busy doing
arku/a (9)	arch
arratsalde/a (1)	afternoon, early evening
arratsaldean (4)	in the afternoon
arreba (1)	sister (of a male person)
arrisku/a (A)	risk, danger
arrosa (7)	rose
artalde/a (12)	flock of sheep
arte (1)	until
artzain/a (12)	shepherd
askatu (A)	to liberate
askatzaile/a (A)	liberator
asko (2)	much, many
askotan (6)	often, many times
aspergarri (4)	boring
aste/a (8)	week
astearte/a (8)	Tuesday
asteazken/a (8)	Wednesday
asteburu/a (8)	weekend
astelehen/a (8)	Monday
ate/a (8)	door
atera (11)	to leave
atsegin (4)	pleasant
atsegin izan (12)	to like, to be pleased
atze/a (9)	the back

atzera (A)	backwards
atzo (4)	yesterday
aulki/a (8)	chair
aurkitu (7)	to find
aurre/a (9)	the front
aurrera (A)	forward
aurreratu (A)	to move forward, to promote
aurten (8)	this year
auto/a (10)	car, automobile
autobus/a (9)	bus
autobusez (9)	by bus
auzi/a (A)	lawsuit
auzo/a (9)	area, district
azken (8)	last, final
azkenean (4)	at last, in the end
azpi/a (11)	underside
aztertu (A)	to examine
bai (1)	yes
baina (1)	but
Baiona (3)	(city of) Bayonne
baizik (5)	but, however
bakarrik (4)	only
bake/a (A)	peace
balio/a (12)	value, worth
balio ukan (7)	to cost, to be worth
baliotsu (A)	valuable
barazki/a (6)	vegetable
barkatu (6)	to forgive
barre/a (A)	laughter
barregarri (A)	laughable
barru (10)	within
barru/a (9)	the inside
bat (2)	one, a(n)
bazkaldu (9)	to lunch
bazkari/a (6)	lunch
bazter/ra (11)	corner, edge
bederatzi (7)	nine
begi/a (10)	eye

begiratu; begira! (2)	to look; look!
behar ukan (izan) (7)	to have to
behartsu (7)	poor
behera (12)	down (direction)
beheratu (12)	to descend, come down
beldur/ra (A)	fear
beldurgarri (A)	frightening
beltz (6)	black, red (dark red wine color)
benetan (4)	truly, seriously, indeed
ber/a (10)	same, identical
bera (7)	he, she, it
berak (7)	they
berandu (3)	late
berde (12)	green
berdin (11)	same
bere (7)	his, her, its
beren (7)	their
berezi (8)	special
bero (5)	warm, hot
bero egin (12)	to be hot (the weather)
berri (9)	new
berritu (A)	to renew
bertan (10)	there, in that same place
beste (2)	other
bete (6)	full
beterik (6)	full
beti (6)	always
bezala (7)	just like, as
bi (6)	two
bidaia (3)	trip, journey
bide/a (4)	road
bideska (12)	path, trail
bigarren (3)	second (number two)
bihar (2)	tomorrow
bihurtu (A)	to return
bilaketa (A)	search
bilatu (7)	to look for, to search
Bilbo (3)	(city of) Bilbao

bilete/a (7)	banknote
bisita (3)	visit
bitartean (10)	meanwhile, in the meantime
bizar/ra (A)	beard
bizardun/a (A)	bearded person
bizi (6)	alive, lively
bizi/a (A)	life
bizi izan (3)	to live
bizidun/a (A)	living being
Bizkaia (4)	(province of) Vizcaya
bosgarren (8)	fifth
bost (7)	five
botila (6)	bottle
buru/a (10)	head, extremity, end
damu/a (A)	regret
den/a (7)	everything, all
denak (10)	all
denbora (4)	time
denbora gutxian (4)	for a short while
denbora luzean (4)	for a long time
denoi (12)	to all of us
denok (9)	all of us, all of you, all of them
desagertu (12)	to disappear
diru/a (7)	money
Donostia (4)	(city of) San Sebastián
duda (A)	doubt
dutxa (10)	shower (bath)
ebasle/a (A)	thief
ebatsi (A)	to steal
edale/a (A)	drinker
edan (5)	to drink
edari/a (6)	drink
eder (7)	beautiful
edo (4)	or
edontzi/a (5)	(drinking) glass
eduki (7)	to hold, to have
egarri izan (5)	to be thirsty
egia (2)	truth

egiaz (2)	truly, certainly, indeed
egin (12)	to do, to make
egon (1)	to be
egongela (11)	waiting room
eguerdi/a (10)	noon
eguerdian (10)	at noon
egun/a (1)	day
egunero (11)	every day
eguraldi/a (12)	weather
egutegi/a (A)	calendar
eguzki/a (12)	sun
eguzkia egin (12)	to be sunny
eguzkitan (12)	in the sunshine
eho (A)	to mill
ehotzaile/a (A)	miller
ehun (12)	one hundred
ekarle/a (A)	bringer
ekarri (6)	to bring
eliza (4)	church
elkarrekin (9)	together
elkarrizketa (1)	dialogue, conversation
emakume/a (1)	woman
eman (12)	to give
enparantza (9)	city square
erabili (9)	to use
erabilketa (A)	use, application
eragin (A)	to promote, to boost
eraiki (A)	to build
eraikitzaile/a (A)	builder
erakusketa (A)	exhibition
erakutsi (6)	to show
erdi/a (9)	middle, half
erdialde/a (4)	city center
erdialdean (4)	in the city center
ere (1)	too, also
ere bai (6)	too, as well (in truncated expressions)

ere ez (6)	neither, not either (in truncated expressions)
erein (A)	to sow
eri/a (A)	sick person
erosketa (A)	shopping
ero (A)	mad
erori (A)	to fall
erosi (6)	to buy
erosle/a (A)	buyer
eroso (10)	comfortable
erotu (6)	mad, gone mad
errege/a (A)	king
erreserbatu (10)	to book, to reserve
erru/a (A)	guilt
ertz/a (9)	bank, riverside
esker/ra (2)	gratitude
eskola (8)	school
eskolara (8)	to school
eskuin/a (9)	right-hand side
esne/a (5)	milk
Estatu Batuak (12)	the United States
eta (1)	and
etorbide/a (9)	avenue
etorri (3)	to come
etsai/a (A)	enemy
etxe/a (4)	house
etxera (7)	home (directional)
etzi (8)	the day after tomorrow
euri/a (12)	rain
euria egin (12)	to rain
euritsu (A)	rainy
Euskal Herri/a (3)	the Basque Country
euskaldun/a (3)	Basque (speaking person)
euskara (10)	Basque language
euskarazko (10)	Basque (adjective)
ez (2)	no, not
ezagutu (10)	to know, to distinguish
ezer (5)	anything (in negations)

ezker/ra (9)	left-hand side
fede/a (A)	faith
fededun/a (A)	believer
fresko (7)	fresh
gabe (12)	without, before (earlier than)
gailur/ra (12)	mountain top, peak
gain/a (11)	upper side, top
gaixo (6)	sick
gaixorik (2)	sick
galdu (A)	to lose, to ruin
garagardo/a (6)	beer
garaiz (3)	in time
garbitu (A)	to clean
garesti (7)	expensive
garrantzi/a (A)	importance
gau/a (1)	night, late evening
gauerdi/a (11)	midnight
gaur (3)	today
gauza (5)	thing
gazte (6)	young
gaztelu/a (11)	castle
gaztetasun/a (A)	youth
gaztetu (A)	to rejuvenate
gehiago (7)	more
gela (10)	room
gelditu (10)	to stop
geltoki/a (4)	railway or bus station
geratu (12)	to stay, to be left
Gernika (3)	(city of) Guernica
gero (1)	afterwards, later
gertatu (3)	to happen
giltz/a (8)	key
gizon/a (1)	man (in general and/or male person)
gizontasun/a (A)	manliness
gogor (A)	hard
gogorgarri (A)	hardening
goiz (4)	early

goiz/a (4)	morning
goizean (4)	in the morning
gora (12)	higher up
gorri (2)	red
gosari/a (6)	breakfast
gose izan (5)	to be hungry
goxo (5)	sweet
goxo/ak (12)	candy
gu (1)	we
gupida (A)	pity
gupidagarri (A)	pitiful
gure (4)	our
guri (12)	to us
gustatu (12)	to like, to be pleased
gustura (9)	gladly, with pleasure
gutxi (4)	little, few
gutxi gora-behera (12)	about, approximately
gutxiago (11)	less
haiei (12)	to them
haiek (1)	they
haien (7)	their
haize/a (12)	wind
haizea egin (12)	to be windy
hamabi (7)	twelve
hamabost (7)	fifteen
hamahiru (7)	thirteen
hamaika (7)	eleven
hamalau (7)	fourteen
hamar (7)	ten
hamasei (7)	sixteen
hamazazpi (7)	seventeen
hamazortzi (7)	eighteen
han (2)	there
handi (4)	big, large
handik (12)	from there
hara (9)	there, to that place
haragi/a (6)	meat
haren (7)	his, her, its

hari (12)	to him, to her
harkaitz/a (12)	rock
harrigarri (A)	miraculous
harritu (A)	to wonder
hartu (5)	to take
hau (3)	this
haur/ra (A)	child, baby
hegaldi/a (4)	flight
hegazkin/a (10)	airplane
Hegoalde/a (3)	Southern Basque Country (in Spain), "the South"
heldu (3)	to arrive
hemen (2)	here
hemeretzi (7)	nineteen
herri/a (3)	land, country, place, village
hi (1)	you (familiar)
higuin/a (A)	disgust
hil (A)	to kill
hil/a (8)	month
hilabete/a (8)	(whole) month
hiltzaile/a (A)	killer
hire (10)	your (familiar)
hiri (12)	to you (familiar)
hiri/a (3)	city
hiru (7)	three
hirugarren (8)	third
hitz/a (A)	word
hiztegi/a (A)	dictionary
hoben/a (A)	sin
hobi/a (A)	tomb
hodei/a (12)	cloud
hogei (7)	twenty
hona (3)	hither, here
hona hemen (1)	here is, here are
hor (4)	there (near the addressed person)
hordi (A)	drunk
hori (5)	that (near the listener)

horregatik (2)	for that reason, therefore
hotel/a (9)	hotel
hotz (5)	cold
hotz egin (12)	to be cold (weather)
hura (1)	he, she, it
hurbil (9)	nearby
huts (6)	empty
hutsik (5)	empty
iaz (8)	last year
ibai/a (9)	river
ibilaldi/a (12)	walk
ibili (3)	to walk
idatzi (A)	to write
igande/a (8)	Sunday
igandean (8)	on Sunday
igo (3)	to climb
ikasi (A)	to study
ikusgarri (4)	worth seeing
ikusi (1)	to see
ikuspegi/a (12)	view, sight
ilara (10)	line, row
indargarri (A)	strengthening
indartu (A)	to strengthen
ingeles/a (10)	the English language
inguru/a (9)	surroundings
inor (8)	anybody (in negations)
interesgarri (4)	interesting
Iparralde/a (3)	Northern Basque Country (in France), "the North"
irakasle/a (A)	teacher
irakatsi (A)	to teach
irakurgarri (A)	worth reading
irakurri (7)	to read
ireki (12)	to open
iritsi (4)	to arrive
irteera (11)	exit, way out
isil (6)	silent
itsaso/a (9)	sea

itsu (A)	blind
itsusi (7)	ugly
itxaron (10)	to wait
itzal/a (A)	shadow
itzaltsu (A)	shadowy
itzuli (8)	to return, to go back
izan (1)	to be
izen/a (1)	name
jadanik (10)	already, yet
jaiegun/a (8)	holiday
jaio (4)	to be born
jaiotegun/a (7)	birthday
jan (5)	to eat
janari/a (6)	food
jantzi (6)	to dress
jarraitu (10)	to continue, to follow
jatetxe/a (4)	restaurant
jatordu/a (6)	lunchtime, dinnertime
jaun/a (1)	gentleman, Mr.
jo (A)	to play music
joan (3)	to go
joateko/a (11)	one-way ticket
kafe/a (5)	coffee
kaixo (1)	hello, hi
kale/a (9)	street
kalte/a (A)	damage
kanpo/a (9)	the outside
kanpora (A)	to the outside
kanporatu (A)	to go outside
katilu/a (5)	bowl
ke/a (A)	smoke
kezka (A)	worry, concern
kikara (5)	(small) cup
kikarakada (5)	a cup full of …
kilometro/a (12)	kilometer
klase/a (11)	class
koaderno/a (2)	notebook
koilara (6)	spoon

konkor/ra (A)	hunch
konpondu (A)	to repair, to fix
kotxe/a (10)	car, automobile
kutsatu (A)	to contaminate, to infect
labur (4)	short
lagun/a (2)	friend (boy or girl), companion
laino/a (12)	mist, fog
lan/a (8)	work, task
lan egin (8)	to work
landare/a (7)	plant
lanegun/a (8)	working day
lantegi/a (A)	workshop
larunbat/a (8)	Saturday
larunbatean (8)	on Saturday
lasai (10)	easy, at ease
lasai egon (10)	to be comfortable, to feel at ease
laster (1)	soon, shortly
lau (7)	four
laugarren (8)	fourth
laurden/a (11)	one quarter
lehen (1)	first
lehen (6)	before
lehenik (4)	first(ly), in the first place, before
lehor (A)	dry
lehortu (A)	to dry up
leihatila (10)	box-office window, counter
leku/a (9)	place
lente/a (10)	lens
letra (11)	letter (sign)
libre (8)	free
liburu/a (2)	book
liburutegi/a (A)	bookcase, library
loradenda (7)	florist (store)
lore/a (7)	flower
lurrin/a (A)	vapor
lurrindu (A)	to evaporate
luze (4)	long

mahai/a (6)	table
mahaian (6)	on the table
maite (A)	beloved
maitetasun/a (A)	love
mendi/a (9)	mountain(s)
mendialde/a (9)	countryside, in the mountains
merke (7)	cheap
Miarritze (4)	(city of) Biarritz
mila (12)	one thousand
mintzatu (10)	to speak (intransitive!)
modu/a (2)	way, manner
mozkor (A)	drunk
mutil/a (1)	boy
nahi ukan (izan) (5)	to want
nahiko (7)	enough, sufficient
nazioarteko (10)	international
neba (1)	brother (of a female person)
negar/ra (A)	tear
nekagarri (4)	fatiguing
nekatu (4)	tired
nekaturik (2)	tired
neska (1)	girl
ni (1)	I
nire (1)	my
niri (12)	to me
noiz (3)	when
nola (2)	how
nolako (5)	what kind of
nolakotasun/a (A)	quality
non (2)	where
nondik (4)	from where
nongo (3)	from where, originating
nor (1)	who
nora (4)	where to
odol/a (A)	blood
ogi/a (5)	bread
ohe/a (A)	bed
oin/a (9)	foot

oin/a (10)	floor
oinez (9)	on foot, walking
olio/a (A)	oil
on (1)	good
ondo (2)	well, fine
ondo/a (11)	side, vicinity
ongi (3)	well
oraindik (4)	still
oraindik ez (6)	not yet
oraintxe (9)	right now
ordea (2)	on the contrary
ordu/a (10)	hour
ordu (erdi) batez (11)	for (half) an hour
orduan (4)	then, so
ordutegi/a (11)	timetable
oroitarri/a (9)	monument, statue
oso (1)	very
oso (6)	complete, total
osotasun/a (A)	totality
ostegun/a (8)	Thursday
ostiral/a (8)	Friday
pagatu (A)	to pay
pantaila (11)	screen
pare/a (11)	facing side
pasatu (11)	to pass
pastel/a (5)	cake
pilotaleku/a (9)	jai alai court
plater/a (6)	dish
pobre (A)	poor
polit (1)	nice, pretty
poz/a (A)	joy
pozik (1)	glad
presaka (10)	hurried, in a hurry
presaka ibili (10)	to be in a hurry
prest (6)	ready
prestatu (6)	to prepare
sagardo/a (6)	cider
sakela (7)	pocket

sakelan (7)	in the pocket
saldu (7)	to sell
saltzaile/a (7)	salesperson
samar (4)	rather, somewhat
sardeska (6)	fork
sarrera (11)	entrance
sei (7)	six
seigarren (8)	sixth
sendatu (A)	to heal
sendatzaile/a (A)	healer
su/a (A)	fire
sukalde/a (6)	kitchen
sukaldean (6)	in the kitchen
te/a (5)	tea
teatro/a (9)	theater
telebista (10)	television
telefono/a (10)	telephone
telefonoz (10)	by phone
tira (6)	look at that!, wow!
trabatu (A)	to hinder, to obstruct
tren/a (3)	train
trenez (3)	by train
txabola (12)	(shepherd's) cabin
txakur/ra (12)	dog
txango/a (12)	excursion, outing
txanpon/a (7)	coin
txartel/a (10)	ticket
txiki (4)	small, little
ugari (A)	abundant
untzi/a (10)	ship
ur/a (5)	water
urduri (A)	nervous
urdurigarri (A)	worrying
urrun/a (12)	distant place
urruti (9)	far away
urtaro/a (8)	season
urte/a (7)	year
utzi (6)	to leave

zabal (9)	broad, wide
zabaltasun/a (A)	width, openness
zahar (6)	old
zaldi/a (11)	horse
zaldun/a (A)	knight
zarata (A)	noise
zaratatsu (A)	noisy
zati/a (5)	piece, part
zazpi (7)	seven
zazpigarren (8)	seventh
zein (10)	which
zelai/a (12)	pasture, field
zenbat (7)	how much, how many
zentzu/a (A)	sense
zer (2)	what
zerbait (5)	something
zergatik (11)	why
zizka-mizkak (6)	appetizers
zoragarri (12)	fantastic
zortzi (7)	eight
zortzigarren (8)	eighth
zu (1)	you (common singular)
zubi/a (9)	bridge
zuei (12)	to you (plural)
zuek (1)	you (plural)
zuen (10)	your (of more persons)
zure (1)	your (of one person)
zuri (2)	white
zuri (12)	to you (singular)
zuzendu (A)	to correct

GLOSSARY ENGLISH-BASQUE

GLOSSARY ENGLISH-BASQUE

The numbers in brackets after the translation in Basque refer to the lesson in which the word appeared for the first time; (A) refers to the appendix A.

a(n)	bat (2)
about (approximately)	gutxi gora-behera (12)
abundance	ugaritasun/a (A)
abundant	ugari (A)
activity	ariketa (A)
afternoon (early evening)	arratsalde/a (1)
afternoon, in the	arratsaldean (4)
afterwards	gero (1)
age	adin/a (A)
air	aire/a (10)
airplane	abioi/a (3), hegazkin/a (10)
airplane, by	abioiz (3)
alive	bizi (6)
all	den/ak (10)
already	jadanik (10)
also	ere (1), ere bai (6)
alteration	aldaketa (A)
always	beti (6)
America	Amerika (3)
American	amerikar/ra (3)
and	eta (1)
anybody (in negations)	inor (8)
anything (in negations)	ezer (5)
appear, to	agertu (12)
appetizers	zizka-mizkak (6)
application	erabilketa (A)
approximately	gutxi gora-behera (12)
arch	arku/a (9)
area	auzo/a (9)
arrive, to	heldu (3), iritsi (4)
as	bezala (7)

author	egile/a (A)
automobile	auto/a (10), kotxe/a (10)
avenue	etorbide/a (9)
baby	haur/ra (A)
back (side)	atze/a (9)
backwards	atzera (A)
bank (riverside)	ertz/a (9)
banknote	bilete/a (7)
Basque (adjective)	euskarazko (10)
Basque (language)	euskara (10)
Basque (speaking person)	euskaldun/a (3)
Basque Country	Euskal Herri/a (3)
Basque Country (French North)	Iparralde/a (3)
Basque Country (Spanish South)	Hegoalde/a (3)
Bayonne	Baiona (3)
be, to	izan (1), egon (1)
be busy doing, to	aritu (A)
beard	bizar/ra (A)
bearded	bizartsu (A)
bearded (person)	bizardun/a (A)
beautiful	eder (7)
beauty	edertasun/a (A)
bed	ohe/a (A)
beer	garagardo/a (6)
before	lehenik (4), lehen (6)
before (earlier than)	gabe (12)
believer	fededun/a (A)
beloved	maite (A)
Biarritz	Miarritze (4)
big	handi (4)
Bilbao	Bilbo (3)
birthday	jaiotegun/a (7)
black	beltz (6)
blind	itsu (A)

blindness	itsutasun/a (A)
blood	odol/a (A)
bloody	odoltsu (A)
book	liburu/a (2)
book, to	erreserbatu (10)
bookcase	liburutegi/a (A)
boost, to	eragin (A)
boring	aspergarri (4)
born, to be	jaio (4)
bottle	botila (6)
bowl	katilu/a (5)
boy	mutil/a (1)
bread	ogi/a (5)
breakfast	gosari/a (6)
bridge	zubi/a (9)
bring, to	ekarri (6)
bringer	ekarle/a (A)
broad	zabal (9)
brother (of a female person)	neba (1)
build, to	eraiki (A)
builder	eraikitzaile/a (A)
bus	autobus/a (9)
bus, by	autobusez (9)
but	baina (1), baizik (5)
buy, to	erosi (6)
buyer	erosle/a (A)
bye	agur (1)
cabin (shepherd's)	txabola (12)
cake	pastel/a (5)
calendar	egutegi/a (A)
candy	goxo/ak (12)
car	auto/a (10), kotxe/a (10)
castle	gaztelu/a (11)
cemetery	hobitegi/a (A)
certainly	egiaz (2)
chair	aulki/a (8)

change, to	aldatu (A)
characteristic	ezaugarri (A)
cheap	merke (7)
child	haur/ra (A)
childhood	haurtasun/a (A)
church	eliza (4)
cider	sagardo/a (6)
city	hiri/a (3)
city center	erdialde/a (4)
class	klase/a (11)
clean, to	garbitu (A)
cleaning	garbiketa (A)
climb, to	igo (3)
cloud	hodei/a (12)
clouded	hodeitsu (A)
coffee	kafe/a (5)
coin	txanpon/a (7)
cold	hotz (5)
cold, to be (weather)	hotz egin (12)
come, to	etorri (3)
comfortable	eroso (10)
comfortable, to be	lasai egon (10)
companion	lagun/a (2)
complete	oso (6)
concern	kezka (A)
contagious	kutsagarri (A)
contaminate, to	kutsatu (A)
continue, to	jarraitu (10)
conversation	elkarrizketa (1)
corner	bazter/ra (11)
correct, to	zuzendu (A)
correction	zuzenketa (A)
cost, to	balio ukan (7)
counter	leihatila (10)
country	herri/a (3)
countryside	mendialde/a (9)
courthouse	auzitegi/a (A)

cup (small)	kikara (5)
damage	kalte/a (A)
damaging	kaltegarri (A)
danger	arrisku/a (A)
dangerous	arriskutsu (A)
day	egun/a (1)
descend, to	beheratu (12)
dialogue	elkarrizketa (1)
dictionary	hiztegi/a (A)
dine, to	afaldu (9)
dinner (late evening meal)	afari/a (6)
dinnertime	jatordu/a (6)
disappear, to	desagertu (12)
disgust	higuin/a (A)
disgusting	higuingarri (A)
dish	plater/a (6)
distance	urrun/a (12)
distinctive	ezaugarri (A)
district	auzo/a (9)
do, to	egin (12)
dog	txakur/ra (12)
door	ate/a (8)
doubt	duda (A)
doubtful	dudagarri (A)
down (direction)	behera (12)
dress, to	jantzi (6)
drink	edari/a (6)
drink, to	edan (5)
drinker	edale/a (A)
drunk	hordi (A), mozkor (A)
drunk, to get	mozkortu (A)
dry	lehor (A)
dry up, to	lehortu (A)
early	goiz (4)
easy (at ease)	lasai (10)
eat, to	jan (5)

edge	bazter/ra (11)
eight	zortzi (7)
eighteen	hamazortzi (7)
eighth	zortzigarren (8)
elderly	adintsu (A)
eleven	hamaika (7)
empty	hutsik (5), huts (6)
end (extremity)	buru/a (10)
end, in the	azkenean (4)
enemy	etsai/a (A)
English (language)	ingeles/a (10)
enjoy, to	poztu (A)
enmity	etsaitasun/a (A)
enough	nahiko (7)
entrance	sarrera (11)
evaporate, to	lurrindu (A)
evening (late)	gau/a (1)
everything	den/a (7)
ewe	ardi/a (12)
examine, to	aztertu (A)
examiner	aztertzaile/a (A)
excursion	txango/a (12)
exercise	ariketa (A)
exhibition	erakusketa (A)
exit	irteera (11)
expensive	garesti (7)
extremity	buru/a (10)
eye	begi/a (10)
face (facing side)	pare/a (11)
faith	fede/a (A)
fall (drop)	erorketa (A)
fall, to	erori (A)
fantastic	zoragarri (12)
far away	urruti (9)
father	aita (12)
fatherhood	aitatasun/a (A)
fatiguing	nekagarri (4)

fear	beldur/ra (A)
few	gutxi (4)
field	zelai/a (12)
fiery	sutsu (A)
fifteen	hamabost (7)
fifth	bosgarren (8)
filling	betegarri (A)
final	azken (8)
find, to	aurkitu (7)
fine (well)	ondo (2)
fire	su/a (A)
first	lehen (1), lehenik (4)
five	bost (7)
fix, to (repair)	konpondu (A)
flight	hegaldi/a (4)
flock of sheep	artalde/a (12)
floor	oin/a (10)
florist (store)	loradenda (7)
flower	lore/a (7)
fog	laino/a (12)
follow, to	jarraitu (10)
follower	jarraitzaile/a (A)
food	janari/a (6)
foot	oin/a (9)
forgive, to	barkatu (6)
fork	sardeska (6)
forward	aurrera (A)
four	lau (7)
fourteen	hamalau (7)
fourth	laugarren (8)
free	libre (8)
fresh	fresko (7)
Friday	ostiral/a (8)
friend (boy or girl)	adiskide/a (2), lagun/a (2)
friends, to become	adiskidetu (A)
friendship	adiskidetasun/a (A)
frightening	beldurgarri (A)

front (side)	aurre/a (9)
full	bete (6), beterik (6)
gentleman	jaun/a (1)
girl	neska (1)
give, to	eman (12)
glad	pozik (1)
gladly	gustura (9)
glass (drinking)	edontzi/a (5)
go, to	joan (3)
go home, to	etxeratu (A)
good	on (1)
good-bye	agur (1)
gratitude	esker/ra (2)
green	berde (12)
greet, to	agurtu (A)
Guernica	Gernika (3)
guilt	erru/a (A)
guilty (person)	errudun/a (A)
half	erdi/a (9)
happen, to	gertatu (3)
hard	gogor (A)
hardening	gogorgarri (A)
harmful	kaltegarri (A)
have, to	eduki (7)
have to, to	behar ukan (izan) (7)
he	hura (1), bera (7)
head	buru/a (10)
heal, to	sendatu (A)
healer	sendatzaile/a (A)
healing	sendaketa (A)
hello	kaixo (1)
her (possessive)	bere (7), haren (7)
here	hemen (2)
here is (are)	hona hemen (1)
hi	kaixo (1)
higher up	gora (12)
hinder, to	trabatu (A)

his	bere (7), haren (7)
hither	hona (3)
hold, to	eduki (7)
holiday	jaiegun/a (8)
home (going)	etxera (7)
horse	zaldi/a (11)
hot	bero (5)
hot, to be (the weather)	bero egin (12)
hotel	hotel/a (9)
hour	ordu/a (10)
house	etxe/a (4)
how	nola (2)
how many	zenbat (7)
how much	zenbat (7)
however	baizik (5)
hunch	konkor/ra (A)
hunchback	konkordun/a (A)
hundred, one	ehun (12)
hungry, to be	gose izan (5)
hurried	presaka (10)
hurry, to be in a	presaka ibili (10)
I	ni (1)
importance	garrantzi/a (A)
important	garrantzitsu (A)
indeed	egiaz (2), benetan (4)
infect, to	kutsatu (A)
infirmary	eritegi/a (A)
inside, the	barru/a (9)
interesting	interesgarri (4)
international	nazioarteko (10)
intoxicant	hordigarri (A)
it	hura (1), bera (7)
its	haren (7), bere (7)
jai alai court	pilotaleku/a (9)
journey	bidaia (3)
joy	poz/a (A)
key	giltz/a (8)

kill, to	hil (A)
killer	hiltzaile/a (A)
kilometer	kilometro/a (12)
king	errege/a (A)
kitchen	sukalde/a (6)
knife	aizto/a (6)
knight	zaldun/a (A)
know, to	ezagutu (10)
lady	andere/a (1)
land	herri/a (3)
large	handi (4)
last	azken (8)
last, at	azkenean (4)
late	berandu (3)
later	gero (1)
laughable	barregarri (A)
laughter	barre/a (A)
lawsuit	auzi/a (A)
leave, to	utzi (6), atera (11)
left (hand side)	ezker/ra (9)
lens	lente/a (10)
less	gutxiago (11)
letter (sign)	letra (11)
liberate, to	askatu (A)
liberator	askatzaile/a (A)
library	liburutegi/a (A)
life	bizi/a (A)
like, to	atsegin izan (12), gustatu (12)
line (row)	ilara (10)
listen, to	aditu (A)
listener	aditzaile/a (A)
little (not much)	gutxi (4)
little (small)	txiki (4)
live, to	bizi izan (3)
lively	bizi (6)
living being	bizidun/a (A)
long	luze (4)

look, to	begiratu (2)
look for, to	bilatu (7)
lose, to	galdu (A)
love	maitetasun/a (A)
lunch	bazkari/a (6)
lunch, to	bazkaldu (9)
lunchtime	jatordu/a (6)
mad	erotu (6), ero (A)
maddening	erogarri (A)
make, to	egin (12)
man (in general and/or male person)	gizon/a (1)
manliness	gizontasun/a (A)
manner	modu/a (2)
many	asko (2)
meanwhile	bitartean (10)
meat	haragi/a (6)
middle	erdi/a (9)
midnight	gauerdi/a (11)
milk	esne/a (5)
mill, to	eho (A)
miller	ehotzaile/a (A)
miraculous	harrigarri (A)
Miss	andereño/a (1)
mist	laino/a (12)
modification	aldaketa (A)
Monday	astelehen/a (8)
money	diru/a (7)
month	hil/a (8), hilabete/a (8)
monument	oroitarri/a (9)
more	gehiago (7)
morning	goiz/a (4)
morning, in the	goizean (4)
mother	ama (12)
motherhood	amatasun/a (A)
mountain	mendi/a (9)
mountain top	gailur/ra (12)

Mr.	jaun/a (1)
Mrs.	andere/a (1)
much	asko (2)
musician	jotzaile/a (A)
my	nire (1)
name	izen/a (1)
nearby	hurbil (9)
neither	ere ez (6)
nervous	urduri (A)
new	berri (9)
nice	polit (1)
night	gau/a (1)
nine	bederatzi (7)
nineteen	hemeretzi (7)
ninth	bederatzigarren (8)
no	ez (2)
noise	zarata (A)
noisy	zaratatsu (A)
noon	eguerdi/a (10)
noon, at	eguerdian (10)
not	ez (2)
not yet	oraindik ez (6)
notebook	koaderno/a (2)
now	oraintxe (9)
obstruct, to	trabatu (A)
often	askotan (6)
oil	olio/a (A)
oily	oliotsu (A)
old	zahar (6)
old, to get	zahartu (A)
one	bat (2)
one-way ticket	joateko/a (11)
only	bakarrik (4)
open, to	ireki (12)
openness	zabaltasun/a (A)
or	ala (3), edo (4)
other	beste (2)

our	gure (4)
outing	txango/a (12)
outside	kanpo/a (9)
pacify, to	baketu (A)
parking lot	aparkaleku/a (12)
part	zati/a (5)
pass, to	pasatu (11)
pasture	zelai/a (12)
path	bideska (12)
pay, to	pagatu (A)
payer	pagatzaile/a (A)
peace	bake/a (A)
peak	gailur/ra (12)
period	aldi/a (11)
personality	nortasun/a (A)
photograph	argazki/a (12)
picture (photo)	argazki/a (12)
piece	zati/a (5)
pitiful	gupidagarri (A)
pity	gupida (A)
place	leku/a (9)
plant	landare/a (7)
play music, to	jo (A)
pleasant	atsegin (4)
pocket	sakela (7)
poor	behartsu (7), pobre (A)
poverty	pobretasun/a (A)
power	ahal/a (A)
powerful	ahaltsu (A)
preparation	prestaketa (A)
prepare, to	prestatu (6)
pretty	polit (1)
priest	apaiz/a (A)
promote, to	aurreratu (A), eragin (A)
promoter	eragile/a (A)
quality	nolakotasun/a (A)
quarter, one	laurden/a (11)

rain	euri/a (12)
rain, to	euria egin (12)
rainy	euritsu (A)
rather	samar (4)
read, to	irakurri (7)
reader	irakurle/a (A)
ready	prest (6)
rectory	apaiztegi/a (A)
red	gorri (2)
red (dark red wine color)	beltz (6)
regret	damu/a (A)
regrettable	damugarri (A)
rejuvenate, to	gaztetu (A)
renew, to	berritu (A)
repair	konponketa (A)
repair, to	konpondu (A)
repugnant	higuingarri (A)
reserve, to	erreserbatu (10)
responsibility	ardura (A)
responsible (person)	arduradun/a (A)
restaurant	jatetxe/a (4)
restitution	bihurketa (A)
retreat, to	atzeratu (A)
return, to	itzuli (8), bihurtu (A)
rich	aberats (7)
right (hand side)	eskuin/a (9)
risk	arrisku/a (A)
risky	arriskutsu (A)
river	ibai/a (9)
riverside	ertz/a (9)
road	bide/a (4)
rock	harkaitz/a (12)
room	gela (10)
rose	arrosa (7)
row (line)	ilara (10)
ruin, to	galdu (A)
ruinous	galgarri (A)

salesperson	saltzaile/a (7)
salute	agurketa (A)
same	ber/a (10)
same (indifferent)	berdin (11)
San Sebastián	Donostia (4)
Saturday	larunbat/a (8)
Saturday, on	larunbatean (8)
school	eskola (8), ikastegi/a (A)
screen	pantaila (11)
sea	itsaso/a (9)
search	bilaketa (A)
search, to	bilatu (7)
season	urtaro/a (8)
second (number two)	bigarren (3)
see, to	ikusi (1)
sell, to	saldu (7)
sense	zentzu/a (A)
sensible (person)	zentzudun/a (A)
seriously	benetan (4)
seven	zazpi (7)
seventeen	hamazazpi (7)
seventh	zazpigarren (8)
shadow	itzal/a (A)
shadowy	itzaltsu (A)
she	hura (1), bera (7)
sheep (ewe)	ardi/a (12)
shepherd	artzain/a (12)
ship	untzi/a (10)
shopping	erosketa (A)
short	labur (4)
shortly	laster (1)
show, to	erakutsi (6)
shower (bath)	dutxa (10)
shut up, to	isildu (A)
sick	gaixo (6), gaixorik (2)
sick (person)	eri/a (A)
sick, to get	gaixotu (A)

side	alde/a (11)
side (vicinity)	ondo/a (11)
sight	ikuspegi/a (12)
silent	isil (6)
sin	hoben/a (A)
sinner	hobendun/a (A)
sister (of a male person)	arreba (1)
six	sei (7)
sixteen	hamasei (7)
sixth	seigarren (8)
slope	aldapa (A)
small	txiki (4)
smoke	ke/a (A)
smoky	ketsu (A)
so	orduan (4)
something	zerbait (5)
somewhat	samar (4)
soon	laster (1)
sow, to	erein (A)
sower	ereile/a (A)
speak, to	mintzatu (10)
special	berezi (8)
spoon	koilara (6)
square (city)	enparantza (9)
station (train or bus)	geltoki/a (4)
statue	oroitarri/a (9)
stay, to	geratu (12)
steal, to	ebatsi (A)
steep	aldapatsu (12)
still	oraindik (4)
stop, to	gelditu (10)
street	kale/a (9)
strengthen, to	indartu (A)
strengthening	indargarri (A)
study	ikasketa (A)
study, to	ikasi (A)
sufficient	nahiko (7)

sun	eguzki/a (12)
Sunday	igande/a (8)
Sunday, on	igandean (8)
sunny, to be	eguzkia egin (12)
sunshine, in the	eguzkitan (12)
surroundings	inguru/a (9)
sweet	goxo (5)
table	mahai/a (6)
take, to	hartu (5)
take a picture, to	argazkia egin (12)
task	lan/a (8)
tea	te/a (5)
teach, to	irakatsi (A)
teacher	irakasle/a (A)
tear	negar/ra (A)
tearful	negartsu (A)
telephone	telefono/a (10)
telephone, by	telefonoz (10)
television	telebista (10)
ten	hamar (7)
that (near the listener)	hori (5)
theater	antzoki/a (9), teatro/a (9)
their	haien (7), beren (7)
then	orduan (4)
there	han (2), hor (4), bertan (10)
there (directional)	hara (9)
therefore	horregatik (2)
they	haiek (1), berak (7)
thief	ebasle/a (A)
thing	gauza (5)
third	hirugarren (8)
thirsty, to be	egarri izan (5)
thirteen	hamahiru (7)
this	hau (3)
thousand, one	mila (12)
three	hiru (7)
Thursday	ostegun/a (8)

ticket	txartel/a (10)
time	denbora (4), aldi/a (11)
time, in	garaiz (3)
timespan	aldi/a (11)
timetable	ordutegi/a (11)
tired	nekaturik (2), nekatu (4)
today	gaur (3)
together	elkarrekin (9)
tomb	hobi/a (A)
tomorrow	bihar (2)
tomorrow, day after	etzi (8)
too	ere (1), ere bai (6)
top (upper side)	gain/a (11)
total	oso (6)
totality	osotasun/a (A)
trail	bideska (12)
train	tren/a (3)
train, by	trenez (3)
trip	bidaia (3)
troubling	trabagarri (A)
truly	egiaz (2), benetan (4)
truth	egia (2)
Tuesday	astearte/a (8)
twelve	hamabi (7)
twenty	hogei (7)
two	bi (6)
ugly	itsusi (7)
underside	azpi/a (11)
United States	Estatu Batuak (12)
unity	batasun/a (A)
until	arte (1)
use	erabilketa (A)
use, to	erabili (9)
user	erabiltzaile/a (A)
valuable	baliotsu (A)
value	balio/a (12)
vapor	lurrin/a (A)

vegetable	barazki/a (6)
very	oso (1)
vicinity	ondo/a (11)
view	ikuspegi/a (12)
village	herri/a (3)
visit	bisita (3)
Vizcaya	Bizkaia (4)
wait, to	itxaron (10)
waiting room	egongela (11)
walk	ibilaldi/a (12)
walk, to	ibili (3)
walking	oinez (9)
want, to	nahi ukan (izan) (5)
warm	bero (5)
water	ur/a (5)
way (manner)	modu/a (2)
we	gu (1)
weather	eguraldi/a (12)
Wednesday	asteazken/a (8)
week	aste/a (8)
weekend	asteburu/a (8)
well	ondo (2), ongi (3)
what	zer (2)
what (kind of)	nolako (5)
when	noiz (3)
where	non (2)
where to	nora (4)
which	zein (10)
white	zuri (2)
whiteness	zuritasun/a (A)
who	nor (1)
why	zergatik (11)
wide	zabal (9)
width	zabaltasun/a (A)
wind	haize/a (12)
windy, to be	haizea egin (12)
wine	ardo/a (5)

wine cellar	ardotegi/a (A)
within	barru (10)
without	gabe (12)
woman	emakume/a (1)
wonder, to	harritu (A)
word	hitz/a (A)
work	lan/a (8)
work, to	lan egin (8)
working day	lanegun/a (8)
workshop	lantegi/a (A)
worry	kezka (A)
worry, to	kezkatu (A)
worrying	urdurigarri (A)
worth	balio/a (12)
worth reading	irakurgarri (A)
worth seeing	ikusgarri (4)
write, to	idatzi (A)
writer	idazle/a (A)
year	urte/a (7)
year, last	iaz (8)
year, this	aurten (8)
yes	bai (1)
yesterday	atzo (4)
yet	jadanik (10)
you (common singular)	zu (1)
you (familiar)	hi (1)
you (plural)	zuek (1)
young	gazte (6)
young lady	andereño/a (1)
your (familiar)	hire (10)
your (of more persons)	zuen (10)
your (of one person)	zure (1)
youth	gaztetasun/a (A)

BIBLIOGRAPHY

The following books on Basque are recommended for further reference or study by English-speaking students:

On the Basque language

Arana, Aitor, Joseph Conroy and Wim Jansen, *Basque-English/English-Basque Dictionary and Phrasebook*, Hippocrene Books, New York, 1998.

Aulestia, Gorka, *Basque-English Dictionary*, University of Nevada Press, Reno, 1989.

Aulestia, Gorka and Linda White, *English-Basque Dictionary*, University of Nevada Press, Reno, 1990.

Aulestia, Gorka and Linda White, *Basque-English/English-Basque Dictionary* in one volume, Elkarlanean, San Sebastián, 1992.

Morris, Mikel, *Basque-English/English-Basque Dictionary*, Klaudio Harluxet Fundazioa, San Sebastián, 1998.

Trask, R.L., *The History of Basque*, Routledge, London and New York, 1997.

On Basque history and culture

Collins, Roger, *The Basques*, Basil Blackwell, Oxford and New York, 1986.

Kurlansky, Mark, *The Basque History of the World*, Penguin Books, New York, 2001.

AUDIO TRACK LIST

FOLDER ONE

1. Title
2. Pronunciation Guide: Vowels, 31
3. Diphthongs, 32
4. Consonants, 33
5. Consonant clusters, 34
6. Les 1 Dialogue, 40
7. Les 1 Dialogue for repetition, 40
8. Les 1 Vocabulary, 42
9. Les 1 Expressions, 43
10. Les 1 Additional Vocabulary, 49
11. Les 2 Dialogue, 52
12. Les 2 Dialogue for repetition, 52
13. Les 2 Vocabulary, 54
14. Les 2 Expressions, 55
15. Les 2 Additional Vocabulary, 59
16. Les 3 Dialogue, 64
17. Les 3 Dialogue for repetition, 64
18. Les 3 Vocabulary, 66
19. Les 3 Expressions, 67
20. Les 3 Additional Vocabulary, 73
21. Les 4 Dialogue, 78
22. Les 4 Dialogue for repetition, 78
23. Les 4 Vocabulary, 80
24. Les 4 Expressions, 81
25. Les 4 Additional Vocabulary, 86
26. Les 5 Dialogue, 90
27. Les 5 Dialogue for repetition, 90
28. Les 5 Vocabulary, 92
29. Les 5 Expressions, 93
30. Les 5 Additional Vocabulary, 103
31. Les 6 Dialogue, 108
32. Les 6 Dialogue for repetition, 108
33. Les 6 Vocabulary, 110
34. Les 6 Expressions, 111
35. Les 6 Additional Vocabulary, 118
36. Les 7 Dialogue, 122
37. Les 7 Dialogue for repetition, 122
38. Les 7 Vocabulary, 124
39. Les 7 Expressions, 125
40. Les 7 Numerals 1-20, 126
41. Les 7 Additional Vocabulary, 132

FOLDER TWO

1. Les 8 Dialogue, 136
2. Les 8 Dialogue for repetition, 136
3. Les 8 Vocabulary, 138
4. Les 8 Expressions, 139
5. Les 8 Ordinal Numbers, 141
6. Les 8 Additional Vocabulary, 144
7. Les 9 Dialogue, 148
8. Les 9 Dialogue for repetition, 148
9. Les 9 Vocabulary, 150
10. Les 9 Expressions, 151
11. Les 9 Additional Vocabulary, 155
12. Les 10 Dialogue, 160
13. Les 10 Dialogue for repetition, 160
14. Les 10 Vocabulary, 162
15. Les 10 Expressions, 163
16. Les 10 Additional Vocabulary, 167
17. Les 11 Dialogue, 172
18. Les 11 Dialogue for repetition, 172
19. Les 11 Vocabulary, 174
20. Les 11 Expressions, 175
21. Les 11 Telling time-on the hour, 176
22. Les 11 Telling time-half past the hour, 177
23. Les 11 Telling time-quarter past the hour, 177
24. Les 11 Telling time-quarter to the hour, 178
25. Les 11 Telling time-1-29 min past the hour, 1
26. Les 11 Telling time-1-29 min before the hour, 178
27. Les 11 Additional Vocabulary, 181
28. Les 12 Dialogue, 186
29. Les 12 Dialogue for repetition, 186
30. Les 12 Vocabulary, 188
31. Les 12 Expressions, 189
32. Les 12 Numerals 21-100 and 1000, 194
33. Les 12 Additional Vocabulary, 195

AUDIO FILES AVAILABLE AT:

http://www.hippocrenebooks.com/beginners-online-audio.html

www.ingramcontent.com/pod-product-compliance
Lightning Source LLC
Jackson TN
JSHW011355130125
77033JS00023B/703

* 9 7 8 0 7 8 1 8 1 3 7 8 5 *